John Dowson

History of India

Vol. 7

John Dowson

History of India
Vol. 7

ISBN/EAN: 9783337820879

Printed in Europe, USA, Canada, Australia, Japan

Cover: Foto ©ninafisch / pixelio.de

More available books at **www.hansebooks.com**

THE HISTORY OF INDIA

As Told By Its Own Historians

THE MUHAMMADAN PERIOD

THE POSTHUMOUS PAPERS
OF THE LATE
SIR H. M. ELLIOT

Edited by Prof. John Dowson

SUSIL GUPTA (INDIA) PRIVATE LTD
CALCUTTA 12

PUBLISHERS' NOTE

The first ten papers published in this volume are drawn from Vol. VII of the original edition of this work, and deal with the reigns of Shah Jahan, Aurangzeb, Bahadur Shah, Jahandar Shah and Farrukh-Siyar, of the little brief authority of Rafi'u-d Daula and Rafi'u-d Darajat, and of the early years of the reign of Muhammad Shah.

This part of the *Studies in Indian History* is therefore to be treated as companion volume to "Shah Jahan", "Aurangzeb" and "Later Mughals".

The three Bibliographical Notices—*Tarikhu-l Jaunabi; Akh-baru-d Dawal, Tarikh-i Haji Muhammad Kandahari, Fytuhu-s Salatin* and *Tarikh-i Hakiman-i Hind* are works relating to the reign of Akbar and reproduced from Vol. VI (original edition).

Of the next three papers, the first analyses the poems of Badre Chach, a poet, of course, inferior to Amir Khusru. His works attracted some notice at the court of Muhammad Tughluk. The two articles that follow are the works of the editor. The first of these is taken from an article in the *Notices et Extraits des Mss*; the other from the *Travels of Ibn Batuta*, a native of Tangiers, who travelled over the greater part of Asia, and visited India in the reign of Muhammad Tughluk. These articles originally appeared in Vol. III (original edition).

The papers on Fire-worship in Upper India and the knowledge of Sanskrit by Muhammadans originally appeared in the Vol. V (original edition).

The following is a list of articles in this volume with the names of respective writers :

1. Tarikh-i Mufazzali—H. M. Elliot and *munshis*. 2. Mir-at-i 'Alam—H. M. Elliot and *munshis*. 3. Zinatu-t Tarwarikh—H. M. Elliot. 4. 'Alamgir-Nama—H. M.

Elliot and Editor. 5. Ma-Asir-i 'Alamgiri—H. M. Elliot and "LUt. Perkins." 6. Futuhat-i 'Alamgiri—H. M. Elliot and Editor. 7. Tarikh-i Mulk-i Asham—H. M. Elliot and Editor. 8. Wakai' of Ni'amat Khan—H. M. Elliot and Editor. 9. Jang-nama of Ni'amat Khan—H. M. Elliot and Editor. 10. Ruk'at-i 'Alamgiri—H. M. Elliot. 11. Bibliographical Notices—Reprint from old volume. 12. Fire-worship in Upper India—H. M. Elliot. 13. Knowledge of Sanskrit by Muhammadans—H. M. Elliot. 14. Poems of Badr Chach—H. M. Elliot. 15. Masaliku-l Absar—Editor. 16. Travels of Ibn Batuta—Editor.

CONTENTS

		PAGE
1.	*Tarikh-i Mufazzali*	1
2.	*Mir-at-i Alam, Mir-at-i Jahan-numa*	5
3.	Aurangzeb's Charity	16
4.	Aurangzeb's Habits and Manners	18
5.	*Zinatu-t Tawarikh*	25
6.	*Alamgir-Nama*	26
7.	Illness of Shah Jahan	30
8.	Heresy of Dara Shukoh	31
9.	*Ma-asir-i Alamgiri*	33
10.	Earthquake	36
11.	Outbreak of Samamis (Mondihs)	38
12.	Caves of Ellora	42
13.	Prince Md. Mu'azzam Imprisoned	42
14.	Death of Aurangzeb	45
15.	*Futuhat-i Alamgiri*	50
16.	*Tarikh-i Mulk-i Asham*	51
17.	*Wakai'* of Ni'amat Khan	51
18.	*Jang-nama* of Ni'amat Khan	53
19.	*Ruka'at-i 'Alamgiri*	53
20.	BIBLIOGRAPHICAL NOTICES	56
	Tarikhu-l Jannabi	56
	Tarikhi Haji Md. Kandahari	58
	Futuhy-s Salatin	59
	Harikh-i Hakiman-i Hind	60
	Tarikh-i Haidar Raz	60
21.	*Kasaid* of Badr Chach	61
22.	*Masaliku-l Absar Fi, Mamaliku-l Amsar*	67
23.	Travels of Ibn Batuta	82
24.	On Fire Worship in Upper India	125
25.	On the Knowledge of Sanskrit by Muhammadans	136

TARIKH-I MUFAZZALI
OF
MUFAZZAL KHAN

[This is a general history of considerable length, written by Saiyid Mufazzal Khan. It begins with the Creation, and comes down to 1077 A.H. (1666 A.D.), the tenth year of the reign of Aurangzeb. A copy of the Table of Contents from another MS. brings the work down to the time of Farrukh Siyar. The work is divided into seven *makalas* or sections, the sixth and seventh of which are devoted to India. In the account of Nasiru-d din Kubacha it gives an epitome of the *Chach-nama*, which was translated into Persian under his patronage. It is an extensive work of nearly a thousand pages, seventeen lines to the page. The following Extracts, apparently translated by a *munshi*, have been revised by Sir H. M. Elliot.]

EXTRACTS

WHEN Shah Jahan mounted the throne at Agra, all the officers of State came to pay their respects to him, but Khan-Jahan Lodi, who was one of the greatest officers under the late Emperor Nuru-d din Muhammad Jahangir, did not attend the Court on the plea of illness. This was very displeasing to His Majesty, and when at last he did attend the Court, he spoke in a very disrespectful tone, which greatly excited His Majesty's anger. As a punishment for his insolence, an order was given to level his house with the ground. Being informed of it, he fled immediately with his whole family and property, and attempted to cross the Chambal, but was pursued by Raja Bahadur with a large force. Ismat Khan, the son of Khan-Jahan Lodi, a boy only twelve years of age, came to an engagement with this officer and killed him with his own hand. The royalists, on the death of their general, made a vigorous attack upon the enemy. Ismat Khan was slain, but Khan-Jahan himself escaped and crossed the river.

In A.H. 1040 (1630 A.D.) the Emperor proceeded to the Dakhin, and conquered many places there. The fort of Daulatabad, which was the capital of the neighbouring territory, was taken by Khan-khanan Muhammad Khan.

Such a magnificent and beautiful fort of red stone was built on the banks of the Jumna, that no building like it was ever constructed by any of the kings who had ruled in India. Besides other magnificent works, the Peacock throne was made by this monarch, which was set with all kinds of precious stones. It was prepared at the expense of nine *krors* nine *lacs* and one thousand rupees.

Sa'du-lla Khan and Mudabbir Khan, who were both good scholars, were deservedly appointed ministers to the throne.

Prince Dara Shukoh was married to the granddaughter of Sultan Parwez, and the nuptial ceremonies were performed with such pomp and splendour as was never witnessed before.

The Mosque of Jama' Jahan-numa was built near the fort under the superintendence of Sa'du-lla Khan, at the expense of ten *lacs* of rupees.

Prince Muhammad Murad Bakhsh was appointed to the Governorship of Ahmadabad in Gujarat, with the grant of an honorary dress and some jewels to the value of five *lacs* of rupees; and Prince Aurangzeb Bahadur to that of the Province of the Dakhin, and *khil'at* with a *sarpech*, a horse, and jewels to the value of five *lacs* of of rupees, was granted to him. They were all ordered to go to their respective provinces, and the Emperor himself came to Agra, where he remained nine months, and then returned to Dehli. As he proceeded on his journey, he amused himself on the way with all kinds of sports.

His Majesty had been pleased to assure his mother-in-law, the wife of Asaf Khan, in the days of her pregnancy, that if she brought forth a son, he would make him a *mansabdar* of 5000 horse; and accordingly, when a son was born to her, the rank was conferred on the child under the title of Shayista Khan Bahadur.

About the same time Muhammad Dara Shukoh was declared to be the successor to the throne, and the entire management of the Government was placed in his hands. The charge was accordingly undertaken by the Prince, but Providence had determined otherwise. The country was destined to be ruled by a juster and better prince, and every circumstance which occurred in those days combined to assist him in obtaining the throne.

On the 7th Zi-l hijja, 1067 A.H. (Sept. 1657A.D.), the Emperor Shah Jahan, who shall henceforth be called 'Ala Hazrat, fell sick in Dehli, and was unable to attend the duties of the State. Dara Shukoh, the eldest Prince, intending to avail himself of the circumstance, so managed that no news regarding the public affairs could transpire. This gave rise to great disturbances in the country. Murad Bakhsh, the fourth son of the Emperor, who was the Governor of Gujarat, seated himself on the throne and declared himself independent. Shah Shuja, the second Prince, also followed the same course in Bengal and prepared an army. Dara Shukoh, being afraid of his brother Aurangzeb, prevailed upon the Emperor during his sickness to recall the forces which were with that Prince. His object in taking this measure was first to despatch the two rebel princes, Shuja' and Murad Bakhsh, out of his way, and then to proceed to the Dakhin against Aurangzeb. He took His Majesty to Agra in the very height of his illness, and sent Raja Jai Singh with a royal army, and his own force under the command of his eldest son Sulaiman Shukoh, against Shah Shuja'. He also ordered Raja Jaswant Singh to march with a large army towards Malwa, the threshold of the Dakhin, to prevent the enemy form advancing. This Hindi chief was one of the gratest Rajas of Hindustan, and as he was very nearly related to the Emperor, he had gained his confidence in a considerable degree, and had obtained a few days before the title of Maharaja. * * *

Towards the end of the year 1067 A.H., when, in consequence of the emperor's sickness, disturbances arose in all parts of the country, Bim Narain, *Zamindar* of Kuch Bihar, took possession of the territory of Kamrup, which belonged to the empire of Dehli. It was also at the same time encroached upon by Jai Bijai Singh, Raja of Asam, who always considered his dominions secure from the depredations of the royal army. To protect Kamrup, a large army was despatched by land under the command of Khan-khanan, who, considering the service very important, obtained leave of the Emperor to depart immediately, and left Kblzrpur on the 13th of Rabi'u-l awwal, in the 4th year after His Majesty's accession to the throne, and conquered the city of Kuch Bihar on the 27th of the same month. After the conquest he changed the name of the city to 'Alamgirnagar, and on the 28th proceeded to invade Asam by way of Ghoraghat. After five months' exertions, the city of Karkalu, which was the chief residence of the ruler of Asam, was taken on the 6th of Sha'ban. An account of the immense booty, both in property and cash, which fell into the hands of the victors, as also of the number of men killed on both sides in these battles, and of the rarities and wonders of Kuch Bihar and Asam, togther with a description of the vegetable and mineral products of the country, the manners and customs of the people, and their forts and buildings, is fully given in the *'Alamgir-nama*. When the Emperor received the report of these important conquests from the Khan-khanan, the general of the royal army, he showed great favour to his son, Muhammad Amin Khan, and honoured him with the grant of a *khil'at* in his own presence. The Khan also received a *farman* in approbation of his services, and was rewarded with an honorary dress, one *kror* of *dams*, and the insignia of the *farman and tugh*.

MIR-AT-I 'ALAM,
MIR-AT-I JAHAN-NUMA,
OF
BAKHTAWAR KHAN

THESE two histories, though circulating under different names, may be considered as essentially one and the same.

Dr. Bernhard Dorn, at p. xv. of the Preface to his "History of the Afghans," describes the *Mir-at-i 'Alam* as a most valuable universal history, written in Persian, by Bakhtawar Khan, who by travel and assiduous study had qualified himself for the task of an historian. Dr. Dorn mentions also that the history of the Afghans by Ni'amatu-lla, which he translated, frequently corresponds, word for word, with that found in the *Mir-at-i 'Alam*.

He gives the following abstract of a copy in the British Museum :

"Section I.—History of the Patriarchs ; of the Israelite Kings ; of Lukman and Daniel ; of the Hebrew Prophets ; of Jesus and the Apostles ; of the Seven Sleepers; of some Saints, as Georgius, Barseesa, Samson, etc. ; of the ancient Sages, as Solon, Pythagoras, Socrates, Diogenes, Plato, Aristotle, Pliny. Homer, Zeno, Ptolemy, Thales, Euclid : after that follows the history of the Persian Monarchs and of the Yemen Kings.

Section II.—History of Muhammad. III.—History of the Khalifs of other Dynasties, as the Saffarides, etc. IV.—History of the Roman and the Turkish Emperors, etc. Section V.—History of the Sharifs of Mecca and Medina. VI.—History of the Turkish Khans, etc. VII.—History of Changiz Khan and his successors. VIII.—History of different Dynasties in Iran, etc., after Sultan Abu Sa'id Bahadur Khan. After that, a history of India follows, in which there is the History of the Kings of Dehli, from Shahabu-d din to Ibrahim Lodi; of the Kings of the Dakhin, of Humayun, Sher Shah, Islam

Shah, and 'Adil Shah; of the Kings of Bengal, etc.; of Jaunpur, Kashmir, etc.; Humayun's conquest of Kabul."

Dow also quotes the work as one of his authorities in his Continuation of Firishta, and in the Preface to his third volume speaks of it as being composed by Nazir Bakhtawar Khan, a man of letters, who led a private life near Faridabad, within a few miles of Agra, and states that it contains the history of the first ten years of Aurangzeb.

This latter description corresponds with the *Mir-at-i Jahan-numa* usually met with in this country; and though the name of the author is the same in both instances, it is evident that Dr. Dorn's and Colonel Dow's descriptions of the portions devoted to Indian history can scarcely refer to the same work. The contents also of the several books differ in many respects, as will be seen from the following abstract of the *Mir-at-i Jahan-numa*, which is found in India; but as there can be no doubt that the two works are the same in substance, there is reason to apprehend that Dr. Dorn's description is defective in some particulars.

The *Mir-at-i Jahan-numa* is divided into a Preface, seven Books (*Araish*), and a Conclusion. These are subdivided into several Sections (*namaish* and *pairaish*) and Sub-sections (*namud*), of all which the following is a full detail:

CONTENTS

PREFACE. Introduction—Gives an account of the creation of the heaven and earth, their inhabitants—the Jinns, Iblis, etc.

BOOK I.—History of the patriarchs, philosophers and kings who flourished before the dawn of Muhammadanism. In four Chapters.—Chapter 1. On the Patriarchs.—2. On the Ancient Philosophers.—3. On the Kings of Persia. In five Sections.—Section i. The Peshdadians.—ii. The Kaianians.—iii. The Muluku-t

Tawaif.—iv. The Sasanians.—v. The Akasiras.—Chapter 4. History of the dependencies of Yaman.

BOOK II.—An account of Muhammad, his exploits, his character and miracles, his descendants and wives, his successors and Imams, some of his friends and dependents, the learned men who expounded the religion, the Sufias and Mashaikhs. In thirteen Chapters.—Chapter 1. An account of Muhammad and his exploits.—2. His character and miracles.—3. His wives.—4. His descendants. —5. The first four Khalifas.—6. The Imams.—7. The ten disciples.—8. Friends of Muhammad whose names are given in alphabetical order.—9. The followers of Muhammad and their dependents.—10. The four great Imams. —11. The seven persons who were appointed to read the Kuran.—12. The great expounders of the Kuran, the descent of the holy mantle, the different orders of the sects of the Shaikhs. In there Sections.—Section i. The great expounders of the Kuran.—ii. The preservation of the holy mantle.—iii. The different orders and sects of the Shaikhs.—Chapter 13. The haly men of Arabia and Persia, the celebrated saints of Hindustan, and the Muhammadan doctors. In three Sections.—Section i. On the Shaikhs and the holy men of Arabia and Persia. —ii. The celebrated Saints of Hindustan.—iii. The Muhammadan doctors.

BOOK III.—The 'Ummayides, 'Abbasides, and those kings who were contemporary with the 'Abbasides; the Cæsars of Rum; the Sharifs of Mecca and Medina; the Khans of the Turks; Muluku-t Tawaif. In eight Chapters.—1. The 'Ummayides.—2. The 'Abbaside Khalifas.—3. The kings who were contemporary with the 'Abbasides. In eleven Sections.—i. The Tahirians.— ii. The Saffarians.—iii. The Samanians.—iv. The Ghaznivides.—v. The Ghorians.—vi. The Buwaihides or Dailamis.—vii. The Saljukians.—viii. The Khwarizm-shahis.—ix. The Atabaks.—x. The Isma'ilians.—xi. The Karakhitais of Kirman.—Chapter 4. On the Kings of Rum. In eight Sections.—Section i. The Kaisaras.—ii. The

Saljukians who ruled in Rum.—iii. The Danishmandias.
—iv. The Salikia Kings who governed in Azurbaijan and
Rum.—v. The Salikia or Mankuchákia Kings who ruled
in Azurbaijan and Kamakh.—vi. The Karamans.—vii.
The Ottomans who are called out of respect Khwandgars.
—Chapter 5. The Sharifs of Mecca and Medina.—6. The
Khans of the Turks. In four Sections.—Section i. History
of Turk, son of Yafis (Japhet), son of Nuh, and his
descendants.—ii. Tatar and his descendants.—iii. Moghul
and his descendants.—iv. Lanjar Ka-an and his descendants.—Chapter 7. Changiz Khan and his descendants.
In seven Sections.—Section i. Changiz Khan.—ii. Descendants of Changiz Khan who ruled in Ulugh-yurat, which
was the seat of his government.—iii. His descendants who
obtained the rank of Khan in the desert of Kipchak.—
iv. His descendants who obtained the same rank in the
country of Iran.—v. The Khans of Turan who were the
descendants of Chaghatai Khan, son of Changiz Khan.—
vi. The Shaibania Kings.—vii. The Khans of Kashghar
who were the descendants of Chaghatai Khan, son of
Changiz Khan.—Chapter 8. Muluku-t Tawaif, who
reigned in Iran after Sultan Abu Sa'id Bahadur Khan.
In five Sections.—Section i. The Chubanians.—ii. The
Ilkanians.—iii Amir Shaikh Abu-l Ishak Inju and the
Muzaffarides.—iv. The Kurt Kings.—v. The Sarabdarians.

Book IV.—Timur and his descendants who ruled
in Iran and Turan; the Kara-kuinlu and Ak-kuinlu
rulers; the Safawiya Kings. In four Chapters.—Chapter
1. Timur and his descendants who governed in Iran and
Turan.—2. The Gurganian rulers who ruled in Iran and
Khurasan.—3. The Kara-kuinlu Kings.—4. The Safawiya
Kings who still occupy the throne of the country of Iran.

Book V.—An account of Hindustan; religious
notions of the Hindus; Sultans of Dehli and other parts
of Hindustan, where at present the *khutba* is read and coin
struck in the name of the Emperor. An Introduction and
nine Chapters.—Introduction. On the religious notions
of the Hindus, history of some of the Rais of Hindustan,

and the dawn of Muhammadanism in this country.—Chapter 1. Kings of Dehli from Shahabu-d din Ghori to Sultan Ibrahim Lodi.—2. Rulers of the Dakhin. In six Sections.—i. The Bahmanis.—ii. The Baridis.—iii. The 'Imad-Shahis.—iv. The Nizamu-l Mulkis.—v. The 'Adil-Khanis.—vi. Kutbu-l Mulkis.—Chapter 3. The Rulers of Gujarat.—4. Chiefs of Sind. In two Sections.—Section i. Kings of Thatta.—ii. Rulers of Multan.—Chapter 5. Princes of Bengal.—6. Chiefs of Malwa.—7. The Farukis of Khandesh.—8. The Eastern Kings of Jaunpur. 9. Rulers of Kashmir.

Book VI.—The Gurganians who ruled in Hindustan from the time of Zahiru-d Muhammad Babar to the reign of the Emperor Shah Jahan. In five Chapters.—Chapter 1. History of Babar.—2. Humayun.—3. Akbar.—4. Jahangir.—5. Shahjahan.

Book VII.—Account of Aurangzeb 'Alamgir. In three Chapters.—Chapter 1. His history from the time of his minority to the period ten years subsequent to his accession.—2. His qualities and character; his descendants; the extent of his empire; his contemporary rulers, in five Sections.—Section i. His character.—ii. His descendants.—iii. The extent of his empire with a detail of the Provinces.—iv. His contemporary rulers.—v. The ancient ministers.—Chapter 3. Contains four Sections.—Section i. An account of the learned men of the author's time.—ii. The celebrated caligraphers.—iii. Some wonderful and marvellous occurrences.—iv. An account of the author's ancestors.

Conclusion.—On the Poets, including the Author.

Size—Small folio, comprising 1540 pages, each page containing an average of 20 lines.

It will be seen that both Dr. Dorn and Colonel Dow ascribe the *Mir-at-i 'Alam* exclusively to Bakhtawar Khan; but it may be doubted if he had really anything to do with its composition. There is in fact very great confusion attending the authorship of this work, which ought, I believe, to be attributed almost entirely to

Muhammad Baka of Saharanpur, an intimate frend of Bakhtawar Khan. It may be as well to consider the claims of these two, as well as of others, to the authorship.

I.—BAKHTAWAR KHAN. He was a nobleman of Aurangzeb's Court. In the tenth year of the reign he was appointed to the rank of one thousand, and in the thirteenth he was made superintendent of the eunuchs. He was a favourite eunuch of the Emperor, who followed his bier for some paces towards the grave.[1] The *Mir-at-i 'Alam*, of which he is the presumed author, and which certainly bears his name, was comprised in a Preface, seven *Araish*, two *Afzaish*, and a Conclusion, and was written in the year 1078 A.H., the date being represented by the words *Aina-i bakht*, "the mirror of fortune," which also seems to confirm the title of Bakhtawar Khan to the authorship of the work. He died in 1095 A.H. (1684 A.D.). The Preface states how fond the author was of historical studies, and how he had long determined upon writing such a work as this. Towards the end of the work, he shows how many works he had written and abridged; amongst others, which are all ascribed by Muhammad Shafi' to Muhammad Baka, we find an abridgment of the *Tarikh-i Alfi* and the *Akhbaru-l Akhyar*. There can be no mistake about the person to whom it is meant to ascribe these works in this passage, because the same Chapter mentions the buildings founded by the person alluded to as the compiler, and amongst them are mentioned the villages of Bakhtawarpur and Bakhtawarnagar.

II.—MUHAMMAD BAKA. His name does not appear in the Preface to the *Mir-at-i 'Alam*, but in the biography of him, written by Muhammad Shafi, it is distinctly stated that he wrote the work at the request, and in the name, of his intimate friend Bakhtawar Khan, but left it incomplete.

[1] Kewal Khan, in the *Tazkiratu-l Umara*.

III.—MUHAMMAD SHAFI'. He was the son of the sister of Muhammad Baka, and he tells us in the Preface to the *Mir-at-i Jahan-numa* that Muhammad Baka had left several sheets of an historical work incomplete, ill-arranged, and requiring revision, and that he was thinking of putting them into shape and rendering them fit for publication, when he was warned in a dream that it was a sacred duty he should fulfil towards his uncle's memory, that he readily obeyed this injunction, and after supplying what was defective in the work, especially on the subject of the Prophets, completed his labours in 1095 A.H., the year of Bakhtawar Khan's death; but after it, because he speaks of him under a title used only after death, and called his work *Mir-at-i Jahan-numa*. This is the history of which the deailed contents are given above. The lose sheets he alludes to are evidently the *Mir-at-i' Alam*, though he does not expressly say so, even when he mentions that work as one of those composed by Muhammad Baka; nevertheless, as the very words of *Mir-at-i 'Alam* and the *Mir-at-i Jahan-numa* are identical in the chapters which relate to the same subjects, there can be no doubt that "the lose sheets" and the *Mir-at-i 'Alam* are also the same; but why the credit of the *Mir-at-i 'Alam* should be so depreciated it is not easy to say, except it was done for the purpose of enhancing the merit of the nephew's labours.

IV.—MUHAMMAD RIZA. He was younger brother of Muhammad Baka. His concern in the work is very incomprehensible, unless on the understanding that, according to the usual Indian foible, he had a quarel with his nephew; for he also edited the *Jahan-numa* from "the loose leaves" left by Muhammad Baka, without any allusion to the labours of his nephew. The precise date of his compilation is not mentioned, but that he succeeded Muhammad Shafi' in the work, and must have been aware of what he had done, is evident; for at the close of the work, where he gives an account of his ancestors and relations, he mentioned the death of Fathu-lla in

1100 A.H., a date five years subsequent to that in which Muhammad Shafi' had stated that Fathu-lla was still living. Muhammad Riza does not say he had the sanction of a dream for his undertaking, but that he had long wished to arrange the dispersed sheets of his brother's history, and had only waited for the time appointed by destiny to do so, which at last, notwithstanding the avocations of his official duties, made its appearance, and the result is the *Mir-at-i Jahan-numa*, a name which he gave to the work, in consequence of the implied wishes of his brother to that effect; but as the imperfect work written in his brother's lifetime was called *Mir-at-i 'Alam*, it does not appear why the name was changed into *Mir-at-i Jahan-numa*, a title chosen with some reason by his nephew, because it represents the chronogram of 1096 A.H. The author says his additions comprise an account of the Prophets from Nuh to Muhammad, of the Philosophers, of the Imams, of the Khalifs, of the Saints of Persia, Arabia and Hindustan, and of the Poets. He says he will mention more about his own additions in the Conclusion: but the two copies which I have consulted, one in the Moti Mahal Library at Lucknow, and the other in the possession of Khadim Husain *Sadru-s Sudur* of Cawnpore, are deficient at the end. He designates the history which Muhammad Baka wrote at the request of Bakhtawar Khan, as *Tarikh-i 'Alamgiri*, and not *Mir-at-i 'Alam*; but it is evident that in this case also the "dispersed leaves" are those included in the *Mir-at-i 'Alam*. He divides his *Mir-at-i Jahan-numa* into a Preface, eleven *Araish*, and a Conclusion, and has subdivided the work in other respects a little more minutely than his predecessor. For instance, he has devoted fourteen *namaish* to an account of the *wazirs*, which by his predecessor is included in one, and he has adopted some other minute differences, in order to give an air of originality to his work, and give him a title to independent authorship; but the two works called *Mir-at-i Jahan-numa* may be considered in all material respects the same. Neither of the editors has added anything to the history of Aurangzeb's reign by Muhammad Baka, though he carries it down only to 1078 A.H.

It will be seen, therefore, that the real author of these various works is Muhammad Baka, though he is the person to whom they are least ascribed, in consequence not only of his attributing his own labours to others, but from the prominence which his editors have endeavoured to give to their own names.

His real name was Shaikh Muhammad, and his poetical title was Baka. He was born in A.H. 1037. In his early youth he applied himself to the study of the Kuran, and in a short space of time learnt the whole of it by heart. Having read a few books with his father, he went to Sirhind, where he studied several branches of knowledge under Shaikh 'Abdu-llah, surnamed Mian, and other learned men. He acquired acquaintance with Muhammadan traditions under the tuition of Shaikh Nuru-l Hakk, son of Shaikh 'Abdu-l Hakk of Dehli, and having obtained his permission to teach this branch of learning, he returned to his native city of Saharanpur, and devoted his time to imparting his knowledge to others. Afterwards, by desire of his father, he forswore worldly concerns, and directed his whole attention to worship and devotion.

When his father died, he enrolled himself among the disciples of Shaikh Muhammad of Sirhind, and made in a short time very considerable progress in spiritual knowledge. On again returning to his native place, he led, like his ancestors, a retired life. Soon after, Iftikhar Khan (Bakhtawar Khan)—who from early youth had been an intimate friend of Muhammad Baka, and had attained the rank of three thousand horse and the office of steward (*mir-saman*) to the Emperor Aurangzeb—invited him to Court, and secured for him a respectable rank, which he accepted, but with much reluctance, and owing only to the importunities of his friends. This appears to have been in the fourth year of Aurangzeb's reign. Although he held a high rank, and had public duties to attend to, yet he always led a life of retirement; notwithstanding which, we are told that the Emperor was very favourably disposed towards him.

Besides writing the *Mir-at-i Alam*, he made extracts from the works of Hakim Sanai, the *Mantiku-t Tair* of Faridu-d din Attar, and the celebrated *masnawi* of Maulana Rumi, "the most eminent writers on Divine subjects, who unanimously agree in their religious tenets."

He also abridged the *Diwan* of Saib and the *Sakinama*, and composed a *Riyazu-l Auliya*, or history of Saints, and a *Tazkiratu-s Shu'ara*, or biography of Poets, with extracts. It is probable that much of these two works is comprised in the *Mir-at-i Jahan-numa*, notwithstanding that Muhammad Riza states the loose sheets left by Muhammad Baka to have been deficient in these particulars. The *Riyazu-l Auliya* is an exceedingly useful but rare work, comprised in 380 pages of 15 lines, and its value is greatly enhanced by being arranged alphabetically. In the preface to this work the author distinctly states, that in the *Mir-at-i 'Alam* he had devoted a *namaish* to an account of the Saints, but thought proper to write, at a subsequent period, this more copious work upon the same subject.

He was also an original poet, and his poetical talents are highly praised in the *Farhatu-n Nazirin*, at the close of Aurangzeb's reign.

Towards the close of his life, he was appointed *sarkar* of Saharanpur, where he erected some useful buildings. At the instance of his relations and friends he constructed some houses on the banks of the tank of Raiwala in the suburbs of Saharanpur. He also founded the quarter known as Bakapura, besides constructing several mosques and public wells. He died in 1094 A.H. (1683 A.D.).

Muhammad Baka was descended from a distinguished family. His ancestor, who first came to Hindustan from Hirat, was Khwaja Ziau-d din. He arrived during the reign of Firoz Shah in 754 A.H. (1353-4 A.D.). He was received kindly by that King, was promoted to be *Subadar* of Multan, and received the title of Malik Mardan Daulat.

He was the adoptive father of Saiyid Khizr Khan, who afterwards became King of Dehli. His own lineal descendants were all men of distinction, in their successive generations, until we come to the subject of this article.

The *Mir-at-i 'Alam*, or the *Mir-at-i Jahan-numa*, is a monument of his industry and ability, and though there is little of novelty, except the account of the first ten years of Aurangzeb's reign, yet the compilation must be considered useful and comprehensive. The accounts of the Poets and Saints are very copious, and among the best to which reference can be made.* It is doubtful how far these portions are to be attributed to his pen. They form, certainly, no portion of the *Mir-at-i 'Alam*.

Several works have been formed on the same model as the *Mir-at-i Jahan-numa*, and continuations of the work are occasionally met with, which add to the confusion attending the inquiry respecting the original authorship. There is, for instance, in the Library of Nawab Siraju-l Mulk, ex-minister of Haidarabad, a large volume styled the *Tarikh-i 'Alamgir-nama*, continued down to the reign of Muhammad Shah, subdivided in the same way into *Araish* and *Namaish*, etc., all taken from the *Mir-at-i Jahan-numa*. The continuation is extracted from the *Tarikh-i Chaghatai*.

This work is not common in India, at least in a perfect form. That of Muhammad Shafi is the least rare, and the best copy I have seen is in the possession of Saiyid Muhammad Riza, *Sadru-s Sudur* of 'Aligarh, though it is not uniformly written. It is enriched by some marginal notes written in A.H. 1216 by a person who calls himself Muhammad bin 'Abdu-llah. In Europe, besides the copy in the British Museum mentioned above, there is the copy in the Bibliotheque Nationale, *fonds Gentil*, No. 48; and the copy of Sir W. Ouseley numbered 305 and 306 in his Catalogue. He observes that he never saw another copy. [There is also a copy in the Library of the Royal Asiatic Society,* of which Morley has given a full account.]

* Catalogue, p. 52.

The cleanest copy I have seen of this work is in the Library of Muzaffar Husain Khan, a landed proprietor in the Lower Doab. There is a very good copy of the work in the possession of Fakir Nuru-d din of Lahore, and a good copy of the first half of the work is in the Library of Nawab 'Ali Muhammad Khan of Jhajjar.

EXTRACTS
Aurangzeb's Charity

When it was reported to His Majesty Aurangzeb, that in the reign of his father every year a sum of seventy-nine thousand *rupees* was distributed through the *Sadru-s Sudur* amongst the poor during five months of the year— —viz. twelve thousand *rupees* in each of the months of Muharram and Rabi'u-l awwal, ten thousand in Rajab, fifteen thousand in Sha'ban, and thirty thousand in the sacred month of Ramazan,—and that during the remaining seven months no sum was distributed in charity,— His Majesty ordered the *Sadru-s Sudur* and other accountants of the household expenses, that with regard to those five months they should observe the same rule, and in each of the other months also they should give ten thousand *rupees* to be distributed among the poor; so that the annual sum expended in charity, including the increase which was now made, amounted to one *lac* and forty-nine thousand *rupees*.

The Habits and Manners of the Emperor Aurangzeb

Be it known to the readers that this humble slave of the Almighty is going to describe in a correct manner the excellent character, the worthy habits and the refined morals of this most virtuous monarch, Abu-l Muzaffar Muhiu-d din Muhammad Aurangzeb 'Alamgir, according as he has witnessed them with his own eyes. The Emperor, a great worshipper of God by natural propensity, is remarkable for his rigid attachment to religion. He is a follower of the doctrines of the Imam Abu Hanifa (may God be pleased with him!), and establishes the five fundamental doctrines of the *Kanz*. Having made his ablutions, he always occupies a great part of his time in adoration of the Deity, and says the usual prayers, first in the *masjid* and then at home, both in congregation and in private, with the most heartfelt devotion. He keeps the appointed fasts on Fridays and other sacred days, and he reads the Friday prayers in the *Jami' masjid* with the common people of the Muhammadan faith. He keeps vigils during the whole of the sacred nights, and with the light of the favour of God illumines the lamps of religion and prosperity. From his great piety, he passes whole nights in the Mosque which is in his palace, and keeps company with men of devotion. In privacy he never sits on a throne. He gave away in alms before his accession a portion of his allowance of lawful food and clothing, and now devotes to the same purpose the income of a few villages in the district of Dehli, and the proceeds of two or three salt-producing tracts, which are appropriated to his privy purse. The Princes also follow the same example. During the whole month of Ramazan he keeps fast, says the prayers appointed for that month, and reads the holy Kuran in the assembly of religious and learned men, with whom he sits for that purpose during six, and sometimes nine hours of the night. During the last ten days of the month, he performs worship in the mosque, and although, on account of several obstacles, he is unable to proceed on a pilgrimage to Mecca, yet the care which he takes to promote facilities for pilgrims to that holy place may be considered equivalent to the pilgrimage.

From the dawn of his understanding he has always refrained from prohibited meats and practices, and from his great holiness has adopted nothing but that which is pure and lawful. Though he has collected at the foot of his throne those who inspire ravishment in joyous assemblies of pleasure, in the shape of singers who possess lovely voices and clever instrumental performers, and in the commencement of his reign sometimes used to hear them sing and play, and though he himself understands music well, yet now for several years past, on account of his great restraint and self-denial, and observance of the tenets of the great Imam (Shafi'i), (may God's mercy be on him !), he entirely abstains from this amusement. If any of the singers and musicians becomes ashamed of his calling, he makes an allowance for him or grants him land for his maintenance.

He never puts on the clothes prohibited by religion, nor does he ever use vessels of silver or gold. In his sacred Court no improper conversation, no word of backbiting or falsehood, is allowed. His courtiers, on whom his light is reflected, are cautioned that if they have to say anything which might injure the character of an absent man, they should express themselves in decorous language and at full detail. He appears two or three times every day in his court of audience with a pleasing countenance and mild look, to dispense justice to complainants who come in numbers without any hindrance, and as he listens to them with great attention, they make their representations without any fear or hesitation, and obtain redress from his impartiality. If any person talks too much, or acts in an improper manner, he is never displeased, and he never knits his brows. His courtiers have often desired to prohibit people from showing so much boldness, but he remarks that by bearing their very words, and seeing their gestures, he acquires a habit of forbearance and tolerance. All bad characters are expelled from the city of Debli, and the same is ordered to be done in all places throughout the whole empire. The duties of preserving order and regularity among the people are very efficiently attended to, and throughout the empire, notwithstanding its great extent, nothing can be done without meeting with the due punishment enjoined by the Muhammadan law. Under the dictates of anger and passion he never issues orders of death. In consideration of their rank and merit, he shows much honour and respect to the Saiyids, saints and learned men, and through his cordial and liberal exertions, the sublime doctrines of Hanifa and of our pure religion have obtained such prevalence throughout the wide territories of Hindustan as they never had in the reign of any former king.

Hindu writers have been entirely excluded from holding public offices, and all the worshipping places of the infidels and the great temples of these infamous people have been thrown down and destroyed in a manner which excites astonishment at the successful completion of so difficult a task. His Majesty personally teaches the sacred *kalima* to many infidels with success, and invests them with *khil'ats* and other favours. Alms and donations are given by this fountain of generosity in such abundance, that the emperors of past ages did not give even a hundredth part of the amount. In the sacred month of Ramazan sixty thousand rupees,[2] and in the other months less than that amount, are distributed among the poor. Several eating houses have been established in the capital and other cities, at which food is served out to the helpless and poor, and in places where there were no caravanserais for the lodging of the travellers, they have been built by the Emperor. All the mosques in the empire are repaired at the public expense. *Imams*, criers to the daily prayers, and readers of the *khutba*, have been appointed to each of them, so that a large sum of money has been and is still laid out in these disbursements. In all the cities and towns of this extensive country pensions and allowances and lands have been given to learned men and professors, and stipends have been fixed for scholars according to their abilities and qualifications.

As it is a great object with this Emperor that all Muhammadans should follow the principles of the religion as expounded by the most competent law officers and the followers of the Hanifi persuasion, and as these principles, in consequence of the different opinions of the *kazis* and *muftis* which have been delivered without any

---

[2] This is double the amount mentioned a little above.

authority, could not be distinctly and clearly learnt, and as there was no book which embodied them all, and as until many books had been collected and a man had obtained sufficient leisure, means and knowledge of theological subjects, he could not satisfy his inquiries on any disputed point, therefore His Majesty, the protector of the faith, determined that a body of eminently learned and able men of Hindustan should take up the voluminous and most trustworthy works which were collected in the royal library, and having made a digest of them, compose a book which might form a standard canon of the law, and afford to all an easy and available means of ascertaining the proper and authoritative interpretation. The chief conductor of this difficult undertaking was the most learned man of the time, Shaikh Nizam, and all the members of the society were very handsomely and liberally paid, so that up to the present time a sum of about two hundred thousand rupees has been expended in this valuable compilation, which contains more than one hundred thousand lines. When the work, with God's pleasure, is completed, it will be for all the world the standard exposition of the law, and render every one independent of Muhammadan doctors.[4] Another excellence attending this design is, that, with a view to afford facility to all, the possessor of perfections, Chulpi 'Abdu-llah, son of the great and the most celebrated Maulana 'Abdu-l-Hakim of Sialkot, and his several pupils have been ordered to translate the work into Persian.

Among the greatest liberalities of this king of the faithful is this, that he has ordered a remission of the transit duties upon all sorts of grain, cloth, and other goods, as well as on tobacco, the duties on which alone amounted to an immense sum, and to prevent the smuggling of which the Government officers committed many outrages, especially in regard to the exposure of females. He exempted the Muhammadans from taxes, and all

---

[4] The *Fatawa-i 'Alamgiri*.

people from certain public demands, the income of which exceeded thirty *lacs* of rupees every year. He relinquished the Government claims against the ancestors of the officers of the State, which used to be paid by deductions from their salaries. This money every year formed a very large income paid into the public treasury. He also abolished the practice of confiscating the estates of deceased persons against whom there was no Government claim, which was very strictly observed by the accountants of his predecessors, and which was felt as a very grievous oppression by their sorrowful heirs. The Royal orders were also issued to collect the revenues of each province according to the Muhammadan law.

Some account of the battles which the Emperor fought before his accession, as well as after that period, has been given above, and we shall now write a few instances of his fortitude. At the time when the Royal army arrived at Balkh, 'Abdu-l 'Aziz Khan, with a large force which equalled the swarms of locusts and ants, came and arranged his men in order of battle, and surrounded the Royal camp. While the conflict was being carried on with great fury, the time of reading the evening prayers came on, when His Majesty, though dissuaded by some worldly officers, alighted from his horse and said the prayers, etc., in a congregation, with the utmost indifference and presence of mind. 'Abdu-l 'Aziz, on hearing of this, was much astonished at the intrepidity of the Emperor, who was assisted by God, and put an end to the battle, saying that to fight with such a man is to destroy oneself.

The Emperor is perfectly acquainted with the commentaries, traditions and law. He always studies the compilations of the great Imam Muhammad Ghizali (may God's mercy be on him!), the extracts from the writings of Shaikh Sharaf Yahya Muniri (may his tomb be sanctified!), and the works of Muhi Shirazi, and other similar books. One of the greatest excellences of this virtuous monarch is, that he has learnt the Kuran by heart.

Though in his early youth he had committed to memory some chapters of that sacred book, yet he learnt the whole by heart after ascending the throne. He took great pains and showed much perseverance in impressing it upon his mind. He writes a very elegant *Naskh* hand, and has acquired perfection in this art. He has written two copies of the holy book with his own hand, and having finished and adorned them with ornaments and marginal lines, at the expense of seven thousand rupees, he sent them to the holy cities of Mecca and Medina. He also wrote an excellent *Nasta'lik* and *Shikastah* hand. He is a very elegant writer in prose, and has acquired proficiency in versification, but agreeably to the words of God, "Poets deal in falsehoods," he abstains from practising it. He does not like to hear verses except those which contain a moral. "To please Almighty God he never turned his eye towards a flatterer, nor gave his ear to a poet."

The Emperor has given a very liberal education to his fortunate and noble children, who, by virtue of his attention and care, have reached to the summit of perfection, and made great advances in rectitude, devotion, and piety, and in learning the manners and customs of princes and great men. Through his instruction they have learnt the Book of God by heart, obtained proficiency in the sciences and polite literature, writing the various hands, and in learning the Turki and the Persian languages.

In like manner, the ladies of the household also, according to his orders, have learnt the fundamental and necessary tenets of religion, and all devote their time to the adoration and worship of the Deity, to reading the sacred Kuran, and performing virtuous and pious acts. The excellence of character and the purity of morals of this holy monarch are beyond all expression. As long as nature nourishes the tree of existence, and keeps the garden of the world fresh, may the plant of the prosperity of this preserver of the garden of dignity and honour continue fruitful !

*The Distances of certain places in Hindustan—
The Provinces and their Revenues*

The length of the daily-increasing empire, from the port of Lahori, province of Thatta, to the *thana* of Bindasal in Bengal, is 994 royal *kos*, 1740 common *kos* known in most parts of Hindustan. Each royal *kos* measures 5000 yards, and each yard is the breadth of 42 fingers. Two royal *kos* are equal to three and a half common *kos*. From the capital of Dehli to Lahori the distance is 437 royal *kos*, and 764 common *kos*; from the same city to *thana* Bindasal 557 royal *kos*, and 975 common *kos*. In the same manner, from Lahori to Thatta 25 royal *kos*; from Thatta to Bhakkar 31 *kos*; from Bhakkar to Multan a little more than 99 *kos*; from Multan to Lahore 75 *kos*; from Lahore to Shah-Jahanabad 170 *kos*; from Shah-Jahanabad to Agra 44 *kos*; from Agra to Allahabad 107 *kos*; from Allahabad to Patna 96 *kos* and a fraction; from Patna to Mungir 37 *kos*; from Mungir to Akbarnagar or Raj Mahal 48 *kos*; from Akbarnagar to Jahangirnagar, or Dacca, 108 *kos*; from Dacca to Silhet 87 *kos*; from Silhet to Bindasal 80 *kos*; and calculating every stage at twelve *kos*, the usual travelling distance in Hindustan, the whole length is 145 stages, or a journey of four months and twenty-seven days. The breadth of the whole empire is from the frontier of Tibet and the delightful province of Kashmir to the fort of Sholapur, which in the prosperous reign of this monarch has been taken from 'Adil Khan, a distance of 672 royal *kos*, or 1176 common *kos*; from Shah-Jahanabad, the seat of Empire, to the boundary of Tibet, is 330 royal *kos*, or 577 common *kos*; from the seat of the Empire to Sholapur, 342 royal *kos*, or 598 common *kos*; as was found by measurement which may be thus detailed. From the boundary of Tibet to Little Tibet, 60 royal *kos*; from Little Tibet to Kashmir, 64 *kos*; from Kashmir to Lahore 101 *kos*; from Lahore to Shah-Jahanabad 105 *kos*; from Shah-Jahanabad to Agra 44 *kos*; and from Agra to Burhanpur 178 *kos*. At the rate of twelve *kos* a stage, the whole breadth is 98 stages, occupying a period of three months and ten days.

Under the management and care of this virtuous monarch, the country of Hindustan teems with population and culture. It is divided into nineteen provinces, and 4440 *parganas*, the revenue of which amounts altogether to nine *arbs*, twenty-four *krors* seventeen *lacs*, 16,082 *dams*, or 9,24,17,16,082 *dams*, out of which the *khalisa*, or the sum paid to the royal treasury, is 1,72,79,81,251 *dams*, and the assignments of the *jagirdars*, or the remainder, was 7,51,77,34,731 *dams*.

Details of all the Provinces

Shahjahanabad—285 *mahals*; revenue 1,16,83,98,269 *dams*. *Agra*—230 *mahals*; revenue 1,05,17,09,283 *dams*. *Lahore*—330 *mahals*; revenue 90,70,16,125 *dams*. *Ajmir*—235 *mahals*; revenue 63,68,94,882 *dams*. *Ahmadabad*—200 *mahals*; revenue 44,00,83,096 *dams*. *Allahabad*—268 *mahals*; revenue 43,66,88,072 *dams*. *Oudh*—149 *mahals*; revenue 32,00,72,193 *dams*. *Bihar*—252 *mahals*; revenue 72,17,97,019 *dams*. *Bengal*—1219 *mahals*; revenue 52,37,39,110 *dams*. *Orissa*—244 *mahals*; revenue 19,71,00,000 *dams*. *Kashmir*—51 *mahals*; revenue 21,80,74,826 *dams*. The four provinces of the Dakhin, viz. *Aurangabad, Zafarabad, Birar*, and *Khandesh*—552 *mahals*; revenue 2,96,70,00,000 *dams*. *Malwa*—257 *mahals*; revenue 42,54,76,670 *dams*. *Multan*—98 *mahals*; revenue 24,53,18,575 *dams*. *Kabul*—40 *mahals*; revenue 15,76,25,380 *dams*. *Thatta*—revenue 57,49,85,900⁵ *dams*.

From the concluding Chapter of Wonders and Marvels

Those who have visited the territory of Jakkar⁶ and Ladakh have heard the following story. In these hills there is found a worm which is exceedingly small. It adheres to the toes of the foot, and bites them. No force of hand or instrument is able to detach it, but it increases

---

⁵ [This is probably a mistake for 5,74,98,690.]
⁶ The Lanakar of our maps.

every moment in bulk and length, so that, having swallowed up the toe, it becomes equal to a large rat, and then swallows the whole foot. After this it increases to the size of a dog, and then swallows up both the legs and up to the waist or half the body of the man. Although the people beat it much and try to cut it, yet no instrument or weapon has any effect upon it. In a short time it becomes like a lion, and having eaten the man entirely, goes away towards the jungle or the hills, and then disappears.

ZINATU-T TAWARIKH
OF
'AZIZU-LLAH

This "Ornament of Histories," by 'Azizu-llah, is a mere compilation of no value. The author informs us in his preface that he intended composing a second volume, in order to reconcile the discrepancies which were observable in different histories. Whether he ever did so does not appear, but there is so little critical judgment exercised in the single volume we have under consideration, that the second is not worth the search.

In the preface we learn that the work was commenced in 1086 A.H. (1675-6 A.D.), but passages occur at the close which show that the work is brought down to 1126 A.H. It is evident, however, that the original work concluded with the account of Aurangzeb's children, and that the few last pages, including mention of Bahadur Shah and Jahandar Shah, have been added by some transcriber. In the last volume the date of 1087 A.H. is given, which leads us to conclude that the history occupied one year in its composition.

There is nothing worthy of translation.

CONTENTS

Preface, pp. 1-11. The Creation.—Adam.—Prophets.—Muhammad.—Imams, pp. 12-111. Persian Dynasties.—

Greeks. — Saljuks. — Osmanlis. — Popes, pp. 212-294. 'Ummayides and 'Abbasides, pp. 294-410. Tahiris.— Tulunias. — Ikhshidites. — Ghaznivides. — Buwaihides. —Isma'ilians.—Sharifs.—Saiyids, pp. 410-464. Ghorians. —Afghans.—Mughals, pp. 674-816. Kings of Dehli, from the earliest Hindi period to the time of Farrukh Siyar, pp. 816-996. SIZE.—8vo. 996 pages, of 17 lines each. This work is rare. I know of only one copy. Malcolm, in his "History of Persia," quotes a *Zinatu-t Tawarikh* respecting the Ghaznivides, which he describes as a metrical history.

'ALAMGIR-NAMA

OF

MUHAMMAD KAZIM

THIS work was written 1688 A.D. by Mirza Muhammad Kazim, son of Muhammad Amin Munshi, the author of the *Padshah-nama*, previously noticed as No. LXI. It contains a history of the first ten years of the reign of 'Alamgir Aurangzeb. It was dedicated to Aurangzeb in the thirty-second year of his reign; but on its being presented, the Emperor forbad its continuation, and, like another Alexander, *edicto vetuit ne quis se pingeret*, but not for the same reason. The Mughal Emperor professed as the cause of his prohibition that the cultivation of inward piety was preferable to the ostentatious display of his achievements. Elphinstone observes of this strange prohibition that the Emperor not only discontinued the regular annals of the empire, which had before been kept by a regular historiographer, but so effectually put a stop to all records of his transactions, that from the eleventh year of his reign the course of events can only be traced through the means of letters on business and of notes taken clandestinely by private individuals.[1]

[1] [See more upon this point in the article on the *Muntakhabu-l Lubab* of Khafi Khan.—See *Aurangzeb* and *Later Mughals*.]

This prohibition is the more extraordinary from its inconsistency with orders previously issued for the preparation of the *Alamgir-nama.* The Preface of that work shows not only the encouragement which the author received in the prosecution of his work, but also the little reliance that can be reposed in the narrative when any subject mentioned likely to affect the personal character of the monarch. It is much the same with nearly all the histories written by contemporaries, which are filled with the most nauseous panegyrics, and

With titles blown from adulation.

The historian was to submit his pages to the interested scrutiny of the Emperor himself, and to be guided in doubtful questions by information graciously given by the monarch respecting what account was to be rejected or admitted. As the royal listener was not likely to criminate himself, we must bear perpetually in mind that such histories are mere one-sided accounts, and not to be received with implicit reliance.

After an encomium of the powers of eloquence, the author says that it was solely owing to the reputed charms of his style that he was introduced to the great monarch 'Alamgir, and, after a long obscurity, was suddenly raised from insignificance to the high situation of His Majesty's *munshi* in the year of the coronation. His style being approved by the King, he was ordered to collect information about all the extraordinary events in which the king had been concerned, and accounts of the bright conquests which he had effected, into a book; and accordingly an order was given to the officers in charge of the Royal Records to make over to the author all such papers as were received from the news-writers and other high functionaries of the different countries concerning the great events, the monthly and yearly registers of all kinds of accidents and marvels, and the descriptions of the different *subas* and countries.

The author was further instructed, that if there were

any such particulars as were omitted in any of the above papers, or not witnessed by himself, he should make inquiries regarding them from such trustworthy officers as followed the royal camp, who would relate the exact circumstances; and if there were anything which particularly required the explanation of His Majesty, the author was graciously permitted the liberty of making inquiry from the King himself.

He was also ordered to attend on His Majesty on proper occasions, to read over whatever he had collected, and had written from the above authorities, and to have His Majesty's corrections incorporated. It is to be regretted that Aurangzeb did not here again imitate the example of Alexander, of whom Lucian gives an anecdote which shows that conqueror to have been less compliant with his flattering historians. "Aristobulus, after he had written an account of the single combat between Alexander and Porus, showed that monarch a particular part of it, wherein, the better to get into his good graces, he had inserted a great deal more than was true : when Alexander seized the book and threw it (for they happened at that time to be sailing on the Hydaspes) directly into the river : 'Thus,' said he, 'ought you to have been served yourself, for pretending to describe my battles, and killing half a dozen elephants for me with a spear.' "

The value of the Royal Records may be known from the narrative of an English traveller who visited the Court in A.D. 1609. Captain Hawkins says, "During the time that he drinks his six cups of strong liquor, he says and does many idle things; yet whatever he says or does, whether drunk or sober, there are writers who attend him in rotation, who set many things down in writing; so that not a single incident of his life but is recorded, even his going to the necessary and when he lies with his wives. The purpose of all this is that when he dies all his actions and speeches worthy of being recorded may be inserted in the chronicles of his reign."

"As the history regarding His Majesty's birth and

minority up to the time of his ascending the throne has already," says our author, "been fully detailed in the book called *Badshah-nama*, it was at first resolved that this book should begin with the accounts of His Majesty's return from the Dakhin towards his capital (which took place in 1068 A.H., 1657 A.D.), and it will contain an account of the undertakings and conquests achieved by His Majesty during the period of eighteen years. But the author subsequently thought of writing, in an Introduction, a brief account of the King's minority, because it was replete with wonderful events, and because many conquests were effected during that period. It accordingly commences with Dara Shukoh's assumption of authority upon the illness of his father Shah Jahan, and the means employed by Aurangzeb to cut off his brothers and obtain the Imperial Crown.

[The style in which this work is written is quite in accord with the courtly panegyrical character of the book. It is strained, verbose, and tedious; fulsome in its flattery, abusive in its censure. Laudatory epithets are heaped one upon another in praise of Aurangzeb; while his unfortunate brothers are not only sneered at and abused, but their very names are perverted. Dara Shukoh is repeatedly called *Be-Shukoh*, "the undignified;" and Shuja' is called *Na-shuja'*, "the unvaliant." The work seems to have obtained no great reputation in India. "Subsequent authors," says Colonel Lees "do not express any very decided opinion upon the qualifications of Muhammad Kazim as an historian. The author of the *Mir-atu-l 'Alam*, however, speaks of him as an author of great erudition; the author of the *Ma-asiru-l 'Alamgiri* has made an abridgment of his work the first portion of his history; and Khafi Khan, the author of the *Muntakhabu-l Lubab*, has made the *'Alamgir-nama* a chief authority," though he occasionally controverts its statements. It is well that the book has been so well worked up by later writers, for a close translation of it into English would be quite unreadable. A few passages have been translated by the Editor, but in them it has been necessary to prune away a good deal of the author's exuberance of language and metaphor.]

The history of the conquest of Assam has been translated from this work by Vansittart, in the "Asiatic Miscellany," vol. i., and in "Asiatic Researches," vol. ii. [The whole of the original work has been printed in the "Bibliotheca Indica," and occupies more than 1100 pages.]

EXTRACTS

Illness of Shah Jahan

ON the 8th Zi-l hijja, 1067 A.H. (8th September 1657), the Emperor Shah Jahan was seized with illness at Dehli. His illness lasted for a long time, and every day he grew weaker, so that he was unable to attend to the business of the State. Irregularities of all sorts occurred in the administration, and great disturbances arose in the wide territories of Hindustan. The unworthy and frivolous Dara Shukoh considered himself heir-apparent, and notwithstanding his want of ability for the kingly office, he endeavoured with the scissors of greediness to cut the robes of the Imperial dignity into a shape suited for his unworthy person.[1] With this over-weening ambition constantly in his mind, and in pursuit of his vain design, he never left the seat of government. When the Emperor fell ill and was unable to attend to business, Dara Shukoh took the opportunity of seizing the reins of power, and interfered with everything. He closed the roads against the spread of news, and seized letters addressed to individuals. He forbade the officers of government to write or send any intelligence to the provinces, and upon the mere suspicion of their having done so, he seized and imprisoned them. The royal princes, the great nobles, and all the men who were scattered through the provinces and territories of this great empire, many even of the

[1] [Passages like this frequently occur, but after this they have been turned into plain language in the translation.]

officials and servants who were employed at the capital, had no expectation that the Emperor would live much longer. So great disorders arose in the affairs of the State. Disaffected and rebellious men raised their heads in mutiny and strife on every side. Turbulent *raiyats* refused to pay their revenue. The seed of rebellion was sown in all directions, and by degrees the evil reached to such a height that in Gujarat Murad Bakhsh took his seat upon the throne, had the *khutba* read and coins struck in his name, and assumed the title of King. Shuja' took the same course in Bengal, led an army against Patna, and from thence advanced to Benares.

Heresy of Dara Shukoh

Dara Shukoh in his later days did not restrain himself to the free-thinking and heretical notions which he had adopted under the name of *tasawwuf* (Sufism), but showed an inclination for the religion and institutions of the Hindus. He was constantly in the society of *Brahmans, Jogis* and *Sannyasis,* and he used to regard these worthless teachers of delusions as learned and true masters of wisdom. He considered their books which they call *Bed* as being the Word of God, and revealed from heaven, and he called them ancient and excellent books. He was under such delusion about this *Bed,* that he collected *Brahmans* and *Sannyasis* from all parts of the country, and paying them great respect and attention, he employed them in translating the *Bed*. He spent all his time in this unholy work, and devoted all his attention to the contents of these wretched books. Instead of the sacred name of God, he adopted the Hindu name *Prabhu* (lord), which the Hindus consider holy, and he had this name engraved in Hindi letters upon rings of diamond, ruby, emerald, etc. * * Through these perverted opinions he had given up the prayers, fasting and other obligations imposed by the law. * * It became manifest that if Dara Shukoh obtained the throne and established his power, the foundations of the faith would be in danger and the precepts of Islam would be changed for the rant of infidelity and Judaism.

Mir Jumla Mu'azzam Khan

[After the conquest of Zafarabad and Kalyan, and the return of Aurangzeb from Bijapur, where he had failed in obtaining full success, through the opposition and malevolence of Dara Shukoh, he left *'Umdatu-s Saltanatu-l Kahira* Mu'azzam Khan, with a part of the Imperial army, in the vicinity of Bijapur, to realize a sum of a hundred lacs of rupees as tribute from 'Adil Khan, by the promise of which the retreat of Aurangzeb had been obtained. The intrigues of Dara Shukoh, who did his best to defeat this arrangement, and the mischievous disturbing letters which he sent to 'Adil Khan and his nobles, brought this desirable settlement to nought. His Majesty Shah Jahan, who at that time took no very active part in the affairs of government, was influenced by the urgent representations of that weak-minded (Dara Shukoh), and summoned Mu'azzam Khan to court. In obedience to this order, the Khan marched with the force under his command to Aurangabad, intending to proceed from thence to the capital. This movement at such a time seemed injurious to the State, and encouraging to the turbulence of the Dakhinis. Mu'azzam Khan had no sinister object in proceeding to the capital; but Aurangzeb, as a matter of prudence and of State policy, made him prisoner and detained him in the Dakhin. When Dara Shukoh obtained information of this arrest, his malignity and jealousy led him to persuade the Emperor that it was all a trick and conspiracy between the Khan and Aurangzeb. By this he so worked upon the feelings and fears of the Emperor that he roused his suspicions against Muhammad Amin Khan, son of Mu'azzam Khan, who then held the office of *Mir Bakhshi* at Court, and obtained permission to secure his person. Accordingly Dara Shukoh summoned Muhammad Amin to his house and made him prisoner. After he had been in confinement three or four days, intelligence of the true state of the case and of the innocence of Muhammad Amin reached the Emperor, and he, being satisfied with the facts, released Muhammad Amin from durance.]

Illness of the Emperor Aurangzeb

[On the night of the 12th Rajab (in the eighth year of his reign), the Emperor was suddenly attacked with strangury, and suffered great pain until the following morning. * * The skill and attention of his physicians had their effect, * * and in a few days he recovered.]

MA-ASIR-I 'ALAMGIRI
OF
MUHAMMAD SAKI MUSTA'IDD KHAN

THIS is a history of the reign of 'Alamgir (Aurangzeb). The first ten years is an abridgment of the work last noticed, the *'Alamgir-nama;* the continuation till the death of Aurangzeb in A.D. 1707 is an original composition. It was written by Muhammad Saki Musta'idd Khan, *munshi* to 'Inayatu-lla Khan, *wazir* of Bahadur Shah. He had been a constant follower of the Court for forty years, and an eye-witness of many of the transactions he records. He undertook the work by desire of his patron, and finished it in A.D. 1710, only three years after the death of Aurangzeb. [Khafi Khan, in his *Muntakhabu-l Lubab*, informs us that "after the expiration of ten years (of Aurangzeb's reign) authors were forbidden from writing the events of that just and righteous Emperor's reign; nevertheless some competent persons (did so), and particularly Musta'idd Khan, who secretly wrote an abridged account of the campaign in the Dakhin, simply detailing the conquests of the countries and forts, without alluding at all to the misfortunes of the campaign."¹]

¹ Col. Lees, Journ. R.A.S., N.S. vol. iii, p. 479.

The *Ma-asir-i 'Alamgiri* contains two Books and a short Appendix. Book I.—An abridgment of Mirza Muhammad Kazim's history of the first ten years of the Emperor's reign and the events preceding his accession. Book II.—The events of the last forty years of the Emperor's reign, with an account of his death.

Appendix.—Several anecdotes of the Emperor, which could not be included in the history; and a minute account of the Royal family.

The history is written in the form of annals, each year being distinctly marked off.

Stewart, in his "Descriptive Catalogue," observes of the writer of this work, that "although his style be too concise, I have never met in any other author with the relation of an event of this reign which is not recorded in this history."

It is differently spoken of by the author of the "Critical Essay," who shows a discrimination rarely to be met with in Indian critics. The omissions he complains of will not appear of much importance to a European reader.

"Muhammad Saki Musta'idd Khan, who composed the chronicle named *Ma-asir-i 'Alamgiri*, has not by any means rendered his work complete; for he has omitted to record several matters of considerable importance. Thus, he has not mentioned the dignities and offices of honour accorded to Royal princes, and their successive appointments to different situations, such as might best qualify them for managing the affairs of government. Some he has noticed, but he has omitted others. Neither has he informed us in what year the illustrious Shah 'Alam Bahadur Shah (now gone to the abode of felicity) and Muhammad 'Azam Shah were invested with the high rank of *Chihal-hazari* (40,000); and of many other circumstances relating to these two princes, some are mentioned, and many have been altogether unnoticed. In the same manner also he has treated of other Royal princes.

"Respecting likewise the chief nobles and their removals from different offices or appointments and dignities, some are mentioned, but several are omitted; thus he has neglected to notice the dates and various circumstances of the appointment of *Hafthazari* (7000) of Ghazi'u-d din Khan Bahadur Firoz Jang, and the *Shash-hazari* (6000) of Zulfikar Khan Bahadur Nusrat Jang, two distinguished generals.

"On the other hand, he relates with minute precision some very trifling occurrences little worthy of being recorded in history, and by no means interesting, such as particulars concerning chapels or places of prayer, the merits of different preachers and similar topics, which had been subjects of discussion among his intimate companions. On this account his work is not held in high estimation among those learned men who know how to appreciate historical compositions."

[This verdict of a native critic is worthy of record, although it cannot be accepted. Muhammad Saki has a style of his own which is not difficult, and yet has some pretensions to elegance. The early part of the work is little better than a Court Circular or London Gazette, being occupied almost exclusively with the private matters of the royal family, and the promotions, appointments, and removals of the officers of government. Farther on he enters more fully into matters of historical record, and gives details of Aurangzeb's campaign in the Dakhin, and his many sieges of forts.]

The work was edited and translated into English by Henry Vansittart in 1785, and published in a quarto volume. [The complete text has been printed in the Bibliotheca Indica, and fills 541 pages. A translation of the last 40 years, Muhammad Saki's own portion of the work, was made for Sir H. Elliot by "Lieut. Perkins, 71st N. I.," and from that translation the following Extracts have been taken.]

EXTRACTS

Earthquake

[Text, p. 73.] On the 1st Zi-l hijja, 1078 A.H. (3rd May, 1668), the intelligence arrived from Thatta that the town of Samaji had been destroyed by an earthquake; thirty thousand houses were thrown down.

Prohibition of Hindu Teaching and Worship

[Text, p. 81.] On the 17th Zi-l ka'da, 1079 (18th April, 1669), it reached the ear of His Majesty, the protector of the faith, that in the provinces of Thatta, Multan, and Benares, but especially in the latter, foolish Brahmans were in the habit of expounding frivolous books in their schools, and that students and learners, Musulmans as well as Hindus, went there, even from long distances, led by a desire to become acquainted with the wicked sciences they taught. The "Director of the Faith" consequently issued orders to all the governors of provinces to destroy with a willing hand the schools and temples of the infidels; and they were strictly enjoined to put an entire stop to the teaching and practising of idolatrous forms of worship. On the 15th Rabi'u-l akhir it was reported to his religious Majesty, leader of the unitarians, that, in obedience to order, the Government officers had destroyed the temple of Bishnath at Benares.

[Text, p. 95.] In the month of Ramazan, 1080 A.H. (December, 1669), in the thirteenth year of the reign, this justice-loving monarch, the constant enemy of tyrants, commanded the destruction of the Hindu temple of Mathura or Mattra, known by the name of Dehra Kesu Rai, and soon that stronghold of falsehood was levelled with the ground. On the same spot was laid, at great expense, the foundation of a vast mosque. The den of iniquity thus destroyed owed its erection to Nar Singh Deo Bundela, an ignorant and depraved man. Jahangir, before he ascended the throne, was at one time, for various reasons, much displeased with Shaikh Abu-l Fazl, and the above-mentioned Hindu, in order to compass the Shaikh's death, affected great devotion to the Prince. As a reward for his services, he obtained from the Prince become King permission to construct the Mattra temple. Thirty-three *lacs* were expended on this work. Glory be to God, who has given us the faith of Islam, that, in this reign of the destroyer of false gods, an undertaking so difficult of accomplishment[*] has been brought to a successful termination ! This vigorous support given to the true faith was a severe blow to the arrogance of the Rajas, and, like idols, they turned their faces awe-struck to the wall. The richly-jewelled idols taken from the pagan temples were transferred to Agra, and there placed beneath the steps leading to the Nawab Begam Sahib's mosque, in order that they might ever be pressed under foot by the true believers. Mattra changed its name into Islamabad, and was thus called in all official documents, as well as by the people.

[Text, p. 100.] In Shawwal information reached the King that Shah-zada Muhammad Mu'azzam, under the influence of his passions, and misled by pernicious associates and flatterers, had, notwithstanding his excellent understanding, become imbued with a spirit of insubordination. Prompted by his natural benevolence, His Majesty wrote several letters replete with advice to the Prince, but this alone did not satisfy him—the Nawab Rai, the Prince's mother, was sent for to go to her son, and lead him back into the right path if any symptom of rebellion should appear in him. Iftikhar Khan Khan-zaman, a wise and discreet man, was directed to repair to the Prince, charged with much beneficial advice. He soon reached his destination, and delivered himself of the King's messages. Prince Muhammad Mu'azzam was a fountain of candour; there was moreover no truth in the report; so his only answer was to bow his head in submission. He wrote to his father letters expressive of humility and shame. Unwilling to ever transgress the

[*] Alluding to the destruction of the Hindu temple.

obedience due to his King and to his God, he insured himself happiness in both worlds. The King, slow to anger and prompt to forgive, lavished presents and kind words on his son.

FIFTEENTH YEAR OF THE REIGN

Outbreak of the Satnamis—also called Mondihs[2]

[Text, p. 114.] It is cause for wonder that a gang of bloody, miserable rebels, goldsmiths, carpenters, sweepers, tanners, and other ignoble beings, braggarts and fools of all descriptions, should become so puffed up with vainglory as to cast themselves headlong into the pit of self-destruction. This is how it came to pass. A malignant set of people, inhabitants of Mewat, collected suddenly as white ants spring from the ground, or locusts descend from the skies. It is affirmed that these people considered themselves immortal; seventy lives was the reward promised to every one of them who fell in action. A body of about 5000 had collected in the neighbourhood of Narnaul, and were in open rebellion. Cities and districts were plundered. Tahir Khan Faujdar, considering himself not strong enough to oppose them, repaired to the presence. The King resolved to exterminate the insurgents. Accordingly, on the 26th of Zi-l ka'da, an order was issued that Ra'd-andaz Khan should proceed with his artillery, Hamid Khan with the guards and 500 of the horsemen belonging to Saiyid Murtaza Khan, his father, and Yahya Khan Rumi, Najib Khan, Rumi Khan, Kamalu-d din, son of Diler Khan, Purdil, son of Firoz Khan Mewati, and Isfandyar, *bakhshi* to Prince Muhammad Akbar, with their own troops, to effect the destruction of the unbelievers. The royal forces marched to the encounter; the insurgents showed a bold front, and, although totally unprovided with the implements of war, made good use of what arms they had. They fought with

---

[2] Khafi Khan shortens the first vowel and calls them *Mundihs* —see post.

all the valour of former rebels whose deeds are recorded in history, and the people of Hind have called this battle *Mahabharat*, on account of the great slaughter of elephants on that trying day. The horses of Islam charged with impetuosity, and crimsoned their sabres with the blood of these desperate men. The struggle was terrible. Conspicuous above all were Ra'd-andaz Khan, Hamid Khan, and Yahya Khan. Many of the Moslims were slain or wounded. At length the enemy broke and fled, but were pursued with great slaughter. Few indeed escaped with their lives; a complete victory crowned the efforts of the royal commanders—and those regions were cleansed of the presence of the foul unbelievers. The triumphant *ghazis*, permitted to kiss the threshold, were rendered proud by the praises of their King. The title of Shuja'at Khan was conferred on Ra'd-andaz, with the rank of 3000 and 2000 horse.

[Text, p. 170.] On the 19th Rabi'u-l akhir, 1089 A.H., a report from Shafi'a Khan, *diwan* of Bengal, made known that the *Amiru-l umara* had appropriated one *kror* and thirty-two *lacs* of rupees above his yearly salary. A claim against the *amir* was accordingly ordered to be entered.

TWENTY-SECOND YEAR OF THE REIGN, 1090 A.H. (1679 A.D.)

[Text, p. 175.] On the 24th Rabi'u-l akhir, Khan-Jahan Bahadur arrived from Jodhpur, bringing with him several cart-loads of idols, taken from the Hindu temples that had been razed. His Majesty gave him great praise. Most of these idols were adorned with precious stones, or made of gold, silver, brass, copper or stone; it was ordered that some of them should be cast away in the out-offices, and the remainder placed beneath the steps of the grand mosque, there to be trampled under foot. There they lay a long time, until, at last, not a vestige of them was left.

[Text, p. 176.] Raja Jaswant Singh had died at Kabul without male issue; but, after his decease, several faithful adherents—Song, Ragunath Das Bhati, Ranjhur, Durga Das, and some others—sent information to the King of two of the wives of the late *Raja* being with child. These ladies, after their arrival at Lahore, gave each of them birth to a son. This news was communicated to the King, with a request that the children should be permitted to succeed to their father's rank and possessions. His Majesty replied that the children should be sent to him to be brought up at his Court, and that rank and wealth should be given to them.

[Text, p. 186.] On the 12th Zi-l hijja, 1090 A.H. (6th January, 1680), Prince Muhammad 'Azam and Khan-Jahan Bahadur obtained permission to visit Udipur. Ruhu-llah Khan and Yakkataz Khan also proceeded thither to effect the destruction of the temples of the idolators. These edifices, situated in the vicinity of the Rana's palace, were among the wonders of the age, and had been erected by the infidels to the ruin of their souls and the loss of their wealth. It was here that some twenty Machator Rajputs had resolved to die for their faith. One of them slew many of his assailants before receiving his death-blow. Another followed, and another, until all had fallen, many of the faithful also being despatched before the last of these fanatics had gone to hell. The temple was now clear, and the pioneers destroyed the images.

[Text, p. 188.] On the 2nd of Muharram, 1091 A.H. (24th January, 1680), the King visited the tank of Udisagar, constructed by the Rana. His Majesty ordered all three of the Hindu temples to be levelled with the ground. News was this day received that Hasan 'Ali Khan had emerged from the pass and attacked the Rana on the 29th of Zi-l hijja. The enemy had fled, leaving behind them their tents and baggage. The enormous quantity of grain captured in this affair had created abundance amongst the troops.

On the 7th Muharram Hasan 'Ali Khan made his appearance with twenty camels taken from the Rana, and stated that the temple situated near the palace, and one hundred and twenty-two more in the neighbouring districts, had been destroyed. This chieftain was, for his distinguished services, invested with the title of Bahadur.

His Majesty proceeded to Chitor on the 1st of Safar. Temples to the number of sixty-three were here demolished.

Abu-Turab, who had been commissioned to effect the destruction of the idol-temples of Amber, reported in person on the 24th Rajab, that threescore and six of these edifices had been levelled with the ground.

TWENTY-FOURTH YEAR OF THE REIGN, 1091-2 A.H.
(1680-81 A.D.)

[Text, p. 207.] The Rana had now been driven forth from his country and his home. The victorious *ghazis* had struck many a blow, and the heroes of Islam had trampled under their chargers' hoofs the land which this reptile of the jungles and his predecessors had possessed for a thousand years. He had been forced to fly to the very limit of his territories. Unable to resist any longer, he saw no safety for himself but in seeking pardon. Accordingly he threw himself on the mercy of Prince Muhammad 'Azam, and implored his intercession with the King, offering the *parganas* of Mandil, Pur, and Badhanor in lieu of the *jizya*. By this submission he was enabled to retain possession of his country and his wealth. The Prince, touched with compassion for the Rana's forlorn state, used his influence with His Majesty, and this merciful monarch, anxious to please his son, lent a favourable ear to these propositions. An interview took place at the Raj Sambar tank on the 17th of Jumada-l akhir, between the Prince and the Rana, to whom Diler Khan and Hasan 'Ali Khan had been deputed. The Rana made an offering of 500 *ashrafis* and eighteen horses with caparisons of gold and silver, and did homage to the Prince, who desired him to sit on his left. He received in return a *khil'at*, a sabre, dagger, charger and elephant. His title of Rana was acknowledged, and the rank of commander of 5000 conferred on him.

Twenty-Seventh Year of the Reign, 1094-5 A.H. (1683-4 A.D.)

Caves of Ellora

[Text, p. 238.] Muhammad Shah Malik Juna, son of Tughlik, selected the fort of Deogir as a central point whereat to establish the seat of government, and gave it the name of Daulatabad. He removed the inhabitants of Dehli thither with their wives and children, and many great and good men removed thither and were buried there. Ellora is only a short distance from this place. At some very remote period a race of men, as if by magic, excavated caves (*nakkab*) high up among the defiles of the mountains. These rooms (*khana*) extended over a breadth of one *kos*. Carvings of various designs and of correct execution adorned all the walls and ceilings; but the outside of the mountain is perfectly level, and there is no sign of any dwelling (*khana*). From the long period of time these pagans remained masters of this territory, it is reasonable to conclude, although historians differ, that to them is to be attributed the construction of these places.

Thirtieth Year of the Reign, 1097-8 A.H. (1686-7 A.D.)

Imprisonment of Prince Muhammad Mu'azzam

[Text, p. 293.] Muhammad Mu'azzam, although a prince of great intelligence and penetration, was led by pernicious counsellors into opposition to his father's wishes, and this conduct became the source of much suffering to himself and displeasure to the ruler of the State. For a long time His Majesty, loth that such conduct should become known, closed his eyes to the Prince's proceedings. During his siege of Bijapur some persons were caught carrying secret messages to Sikandar ('Adil Shah); these men were put to death. Some officers also, suspected of evil intentions, Mumin Khan, commandant of artillery,

'Aziz Afghan, Multifat Khan, second *bakhshi*, and the cunning Bindraban, were expelled from the army on the 18th of Shawwal. The Prince's destiny grew dark, and wisdom and foresight quite forsook him. During the investment of Haidarabad he allowed himself to be deluded by some promise of Abu-l Hasan, and at last sundry written communications, which passed between the trenches and the fort of Golkonda, fell into the hands of Firoz Jang. Other proofs were also available of the Prince's treachery. The Khan, that very night, laid these documents before the King, who was now well convinced of the Prince's wilfulness, whatever doubts he might have entertained before. Hayat Khan, *darogha* of the Prince's *diwan-khana*, was sent for and ordered to direct his master to send his troops to oppose Shaikh Nizam Haidarabadi, who was about to make a night attack on the camp. Ihtimam Khan, it was said, would guard the Prince's tents during the absence of his own people. This order was obeyed.

The next morning, according to order, the Prince, Mu'izzu-d din, and Muhammad 'Azim,* attended the *darbar*. His Majesty, after taking his seat, told them that Asad Khan and Bahramand Khan had something to communicate to them in the chapel. No sooner had the Princes entered this place than their arms were taken from them. As soon as a tent could be pitched, they were removed into it. His Majesty withdrew to the seraglio by the private entrance, and there, wringing his hands, and with many symptoms of grief, he exclaimed that the labour of forty years had fallen to the ground!.

Guards were placed round the tent, under the orders of Ihtimam Khan. *Mutasaddis* seized all the Prince's property, which, however, was but as a drop of water in the ocean. Ihtimam was invested with the title of Sardar Khan, and raised from the command of 1000 to that of 1500.

* More commonly called Muhammad 'Azim.

Thirty-fifth Year of the Reign, 1102-3 A.H. (1691-2 A.D.)

Release of Muhammad Mu'azzam from Confinement

[Text, p. 841.] Neither the Prince nor his sons had been, when first confined, permitted even to unbind the hair of their heads. This treatment lasted six months. Khidmat Khan, *Nazir*, emboldened by his long service under this King and under his father, remonstrated most vehemently against this severity (no other dared to speak in the Prince's favour), and His Majesty relented. As time wore on, the King's wrath grew less, his paternal feelings resumed their sway, and he daily sent his blessing by Sardar Khan to this second Joseph, imprisoned like Jonas, desiring him to be satisfied with this much until the Father of all Mercies moved his heart to put an end to his sufferings. Strange to relate, Sardar Khan one day told the King that His Majesty could order the Prince's release when he thought fit so to do. "True," replied the King, "but Providence has made me ruler of the habitable world. The oppressed person appeals to me against his oppressor, and expects redress. This son of mine has endured some hardships at my hands, in expiation of certain worldly offences, but the hour has not yet come for me to release him; his only hope is in God. Let him therefore be hopeful, so that he may not lose all hope in me, nor appeal against me to God, for should he do so, what refuge would be left to me?"

Fate had decreed that Muhammad Mu'azzam should adorn the throne; wherefore the King, that personification of all virtues, resolved to draw the Prince from the state in which he had been kept, and let his light shine on the people. That his mind might not bow down under the weight of grief, the rigours of confinement were gradually made less. On one occasion, when the King marched from Badri, all the tents were ordered to be left standing for the Prince's recreation. He was permitted to wander from one to the other, enjoying the luxuries each different place afforded, and refreshing body and mind. The Prince observed to the officers who had charge of him that he longed to behold His Majesty, and that the sight of such places could not satisfy that wish. At length, when the news of the Prince's mother having died in the capital was received, His Majesty caused a tent of communication to be pitched between the *diwan-i khas* and the Prince's tent, where the monarch repaired in person with the virtuous Princess Zinatu-n Nisa Begam, and offered the usual consolations.

Some time after this, on the 4th of Zi-l ka'da, Mu'azzam had the honour of paying his respects to the King, who desired him to perform his mid-day prayers in his presence. When His Majesty went to the mosque on Fridays, the Prince was to pray in the private chapel. Permission was also granted him to visit occasionally the baths in the fort; at other times he might wander among the parterres and tanks of the Shahabad gardens. Thus by degrees was broken the barrier between father and son. Khwaja Daulat received orders to fetch the Prince's family from the capital.[a]

FIFTY-FIRST YEAR OF THE REIGN

Death of Aurangzeb

[Text, p. 519.] After the conclusion of the holy wars which rescued the countries of the Dakhin from the dominion of the pagans, the army encamped at Ahmadnagar on the 16th of Shawwal, in the 50th year of the reign. A year after this, at the end of Shawwal, in the 51st year of the reign, the King fell ill, and consternation spready among people of all ranks; but, by the blessing of Providence, His Majesty recovered his health in a short time, and once more resumed the administration of affairs. About this time the noble Shah ('Alam) was appointed governor of the province of Malwa, and Prince

---

[a] From subsequent passages it appears that this Prince was reinstated in his seat on the Emperor's right hand in the thirty-ninth year, and was presented to the government of Kabul in the forty-second year.

Kam Bakhsh governor of that of Bijapur. Only four or five days had elapsed after the departure of their royal highnesses, when the King was seized with a burning fever, which continued unabated for three days. Still His Majesty did not relax in his devotions, every ordinance of religion was strictly kept. On the evening of Thursday, His Majesty perused a petition from Hamidu-d din Khan, who stated that he had devoted the sum of 4000 rupees, the price of an elephant, as a propitiatory sacrifice, and begged to be permitted to make over this amount to the Kazi Mulla Haidar for distribution. The King granted the request, and, though weak and suffering, wrote with his own hand on the petition that it was his earnest wish that this sacrifice should lead to a speedy dissolution of his mortal frame.

On the morning of Friday, 28th of Zi-l ka'da (1118 A.H. 21st February, 1707 A.D.), His Majesty performed the consecrated prayers, and, at their conclusion, returned to the sleeping apartments, where he remained absorbed in contemplation of the Deity. Faintness came on, and the soul of the aged monarch hovered on the verge of eternity. Still, in this dread hour, the force of habit prevailed, and the fingers of the dying King continued mechanically to tell the beads of the rosary they held. A quarter of the day later the King breathed his last, and thus was fulfilled his wish to die on a Friday. Great was the grief among all classes of people for the King's death. The shafts of adversity had demolished the edifice of their hopes, and the night of sorrow darkened the joyful noonday. Holy men prepared to perform the funeral rites, and kept the corpse in the sleeping apartment pending the arrival of Prince Muhammad A'zam, who was away a distance of five-and-twenty *kos* from the camp. The Prince arrived the following day, and it is impossible to describe the grief that was depicted on his countenance; never had anything like it been beheld. On Monday he assisted in carrying the corpse through the hall of justice, whence the procession went on without him. May none ever experience the anguish he felt ! People sympathized with the Prince's sorrow, and shed torrents of tears. Such and so deeply-felt were the lamentations for a monarch whose genius only equalled his piety, whose equal the world did not contain, but whose luminous countenance was now hidden from his loving people !

According to the will of the deceased King, his mortal remains were deposited in the tomb constructed during his lifetime near the shrine of the holy Shaikh Zainu-d din (on whom God have mercy!). "Earth was consigned to earth, but the pure soul survived." This place of sepulture, known by the name of Khuldabad, is distant eight *kos* from Khujista-bunyad (Aurangabad), and three *kos* from Daulatabad. A red stone three yards in length, two in width, and only a few inches in depth, is placed above the tomb. In this stone was hollowed out, in the shape of an amulet, a cavity for the reception of earth and seeds; and odoriferous herbs there diffuse their fragrance around.

Account of the late King's Family

[Text, p. 533.] God had given unto 'Alamgir five sons and five daughters, born of different mothers, and all learned in spiritual and worldly matters. Mention has already been made of them; it now remains to give a short notice of each.

The first son was Muhammad Sultan, born of the Nawab Bai, on the 4th of Ramazan, in the year 1049 A.H. (14th November, 1639 A.D.). His manners were agreeable, he knew the Kuran by heart, and was well acquainted with the Arabic, Turkish and Persian languages. His valour was great. This Prince died in the 21st year of the reign.

The second son, Muhammad Mu'azzam Shah 'Alam Bahadur, was born of the same Nawab Bai, in the end of Rajab, 1053 A.H. (September, 1643 A.D.). While a boy he acquired a perfect knowledge of the Kuran, and of the science of reading. When so engaged, his voice is pleasing and melodious. So great is his knowledge of law and of the traditionary sayings of the Prophet, that he is held by all the learned men of the day to be unequalled in this accomplishment. He is deeply read in Arabic, and the fluency and elegance of his diction are the wonder of the very Kuran-readers of Arabia. He knows many sorts of writing, is careful of his time, and a protector of the poor.

Prince Muhammad A'zam, the third son, was born of Dilras Banu Begam, daughter of Shah Nawaz Khan Safawi, on the 12th of Sha'ban, in the year 1063 (28th June, 1653). He was distinguished for his wisdom and excellence. He excelled in many ways, and his innate virtues and sagacity rendered him the indispensable companion of the late King. His death occurred on the 18th of Rabi'u-l awwal, only three months and twenty days after that of his royal parent. It was marked by deeds of valour.

The next son, Prince Akbar, was born of Begam,[*] on the 12th of Zi-l hijja, in the year 1067 (12th September, 1656 A.D.). He fled from his father, and passed his life in Persia. He died in the 48th year of the reign, but there are two reasons for supposing that his end was a happy one. In the first place, the King remarked that Prince Akbar had always performed his Friday prayers most devoutly; and secondly, his mortal remains lie in the area of the tomb of Imam Riza (on whom be blessings and praise!).

Muhammad Kam Bakhsh, the fifth and last son, was born on the 10th of Ramazan, in the year 1077 (25th February, 1667). His mother was Bai Udipuri. His father instructed him in the word of God, and his knowledge of all known works surpassed that of his brothers. The Turkish language and several modes of writing were familiar to him. He was brave and generous. The death of this Prince took place two years after that of his father.

[*] The name is not given.

Account of the Daughters

Zebu-n Nisa Begam was the eldest of the daughters. She was born of Begam* on the 10th of Shawwal, in the year 1048 (5th February, 1639). Owing to the King's teaching, she became thoroughly proficient in knowledge of the Kuran, and received as a reward the sum of 30,000 ashrafis. Her learning extended to Arabic, Persian, to the various modes of writing, and to prose and poetry. Many learned men, poets and writers were employed by her, and numerous compilations and original works are dedicated to her. One of these, a translation of the *Tafsir-i Kabir*, called *Zebu-t Tafasir*, was the work of Mulla Safi'u-d din Ardbeli, attached to the service of this Princess. Her death occurred in the year 1113 (1701 A.D.).

The second daughter was Zinatu-n Nisa Begam. She was born on the 1st Sha'ban, in the year 1053 (9th October, 1643 A.D.). This Princess is remarkable for her great piety and extreme liberality.

Badru-n Nisa Begam, the third in order, was born of the Nawab Bai on the 29th Shawwal, in the year 1057 (17th November, 1647 A.D.). She knew the Kuran by heart, was pious and virtuous. Her demise took place on the 27th Zi-l ka'da in the 18th year of the reign.

The fourth daughter, Zubdatu-n Nisa Begam, was born on the 26th Ramazan, in the year 1061 (1st September, 1651 A.D.). Her mother was Begam. This Princess was ever engaged in worship, prayer, and pious works. She was wedded to Sipihr Shukoh, son of Dara Shukoh. She went to Paradise in the same month as her father, to whom her death was not made known.

Mihru-n Nisa Begam, the fifth daughter, was born of Aurangabadi Mahal on the 3rd of Safar, in the year 1072 (13th September, 1661). She became the spouse of Izad Bakhsh, son of Murad Bakhsh, and lived until the year 1116.

* The name is not given.

FUTUHAT-I 'ALAMGIRI
OF
MUHAMMAD MA'SUM

[THIS book of "the Victories of Aurangzeb" would seem also to be known as *Waki'at-i 'Alamgiri*. There is a translation of the Preface and of the Table of Contents among Sir H. M. Elliot's papers. From the Preface it appears that the author was Muhammad Ma'sum, son of Salih. He was employed in the service of Sultan Shuja', Aurangzeb's brother, "whose generosity is equal to that of the sun." Having obtained a few months' leave of absence, he, with much hesitation and diffidence, determined, as he says, "to write the events of these two or three years, which I have witnessed myself or have heard from others." The Table of Contents gives 55 Chapters. The first relates to Shah Jahan's conquest of Balkh and Badakhshan. Chapter 52 "relates the murder of Dara Shukoh by the orders of Aurangzeb in the garden of Khizrabad, by the hands of Shah Nazar *Chela*, and of the burial of his remains in the mausoleum of Humayun, which is the burial-place of all the murdered princes of this house." Chapter 55 gives the remaining account of Shah Shuja' and Mu'azzam Khan. The translator adds: "The history is not complete, and it is not known whether the author had written only thus far, or whether the scribe had no time to copy further." As it professes to be only the history of two or three years, it is probably complete. There is, according to Dr. Bird, another work bearing this title written by Sri Das, a Nagar Brahman of Gujarat. "The author was a spectator of the occurrences he details, and was in the service of Shaikhu-l Islam, the son of 'Abdu-l Wahhab Ahmadabadi. This work is very rare."[1]]

---

[1] Bird's *Gujarat*, p. 89.

TARIKH-I MULK-I ASHAM
OF
SHAHABU-D DIN TALASH

[THIS is an account of the expedition to Assam undertaken in the fourth year of the reign of Aurangzeb, by Mu'azzam Khan Khan-khanan. The author was Maulana Ahmad Shahabu-d din Talash. It is a small work, and is noticed in Stewart's Catalogue.[1] There are some Extracts of the work among Sir H. M. Elliot's papers, and there is a copy in the Library of the Asiatic Society of Bengal.]

WAKAI'
OF
NI'AMAT KHAN

[THIS is the work of the celebrated wit and satirist, Mirza Muhammad Ni'amat Khan, whose poetical sobriquet was 'Ali. His writings are much valued in India for the excellence of the style, which is highly florid; but it is very obscure, and is more pregnant with metaphor than meaning. The author was appointed to the office of news-writer by Aurangzeb, and the *Wakai'* is especially devoted to the history of the siege and conquest of Golkonda. The *Makhzanu-l Gharaib* states that his ancestors were physicians of Shiraz, but that he was brought up in Hindustan. He was appointed by Aurangzeb to the *mansab* of *bakawali*, with the title of Ni'amat Khan, but he was ungrateful to his patron and satirized him. At length, from improper conduct, he fell into disgrace. "His verses and *ghazals* are not excellent, but his satire is pleasant and pungent." It appears that he had some

---

[1] See *Journ. des Savants*, 1845, p. 702.

knowledge of medicine. The *Tarikh-i Chaghatai* also speaks of his strong powers of satire, and states that he received the title of Danishmand Khan in the first year of the reign of Bahadur Shah. He afterwards wrote a *Shahnama*, and died at Dehli in 1122 A.H. (1710 A.D.), in the 4th year of Bahadur Shah, or according to another authority, two years earlier. The author is the person referred to in the following passage from "The Critical Essay" : "Mirza Muhammad, generally called Ni'amat Khan Haji, was an eminent personage, who obtained the title of Danishmand Khan, and he has recorded the events of that monarch's (Aurangzeb's) reign as far as the third year. Although his work is written in a very pleasing style, yet it occasionally offends the reader's delicacy by indecent jests and coarse witticisms, in which the author was too much accustomed to indulge." In the Catalogue of Jonathan Scott's library, the *Wakai'* is said to be a most curious work, exhibiting anecdotes of private character in a humorous and entertaining style; but, says Sir H. M. Elliot, "I conceive that allusion must be made to the *Muzhakat*, which has been lithographed at Lucknow in the same volume as the author's *Ruka'at*." The *Wakai'* has been printed at Bombay in a volume of 319 pages. It was also published at Lucknow in 1845. The Editor of this edition, after lauding the author in the Preface, says that "the work contains very difficult and complicated passages not suited to the comprehension of common people; so, with great pains and diligent research in Persian and Arabic dictionaries, he has supplied marginal notes, turning the most difficult passages into a smooth and easy style."

There is an abstract of a portion of this work among the papers, but it is a short dry summary of no value, either as a specimen of the work, or as a contribution to history.[1]]

[1] [This article has been compiled from Sir H. M. Elliot's rough sketch and from Persian notes and extracts collected by him.]

JANG-NAMA
OF
NI'AMAT KHAN 'ALI

[This "Book of War" is another production of Ni'amat Khan or Danishmand Khan, the writer of the last-noticed work. An abstract of the work prepared for Sir H. M. Elliot shows that it begins with the war carried on by Aurangzeb against the Rana of Udipur, and ends with the accession of Bahadur Shah. The struggle which followed the death of Aurangzeb occupies a considerable portion of the work. A lithographed edition of the work was printed at Lucknow in 1261 A.H. (1845 A.D.).]

RUKA'AT-I 'ALAMGIRI
OF
THE EMPEROR AURANGZEB

These letters exhibit the private life and sentiments of this Prince, so they should be allowed a place in his history. The following account is given of them by Elphinstone in his History (p. 679).

"There are three collections of his letters. First, the *Kalimat-i Taiyibat*, published by one of his chief secretaries, 'Inayatu-llah; second, the *Raknim-i Kara'im* by the son of another secretary; and third, the *Dasturu-l Aml Agahi* collected from all quarters thirty-eight years after his death. The first two collections profess to be merely the rough drafts or notes which he wrote with his own hand for his secretaries. Most of the third collection have the same appearance. They are without dates or order, and are often obscure, from their brevity; and our ignorance of the subjects alluded to."

One set was indifferently translated many years ago by Eales in Calcutta, and a few Extracts have been published in the Asiatic Annual Register, vol. iii.

Instead of three sets of these letters, there appears to be more than four.

The first of them has the following passage in the Preface: "Be it known to all learned men, that this book named *Ruka'at-i 'Alamgir,* and surnamed *Kalimat-i Taiyibat,* has been compiled from the epistles written by Muhiu-d din Muhammad Aurangzeb, King of Hindustan. The expression *Muhin pur khilafat wa Farzand Sa'adat tawam* has been used in this book for the eldest son of the King, Sultan Muhammad Mu'azzam, surnamed Shah 'Alam. Sometimes the expression *Sa'adat towam* has also been applied to his second son, Sultan Muhammad A'zam Shah; but the term *Farzand-i 'Ali Jah* is only used for the eldest. By the term *Biradar-i na-mihrban* is meant the King's elder brother, Dara Shukoh. The expressions *Farzand-zada-i 'aziz* and *Farzand-zada bahadur* are respectively intended for Muhammad Mu'izzu-d din, the eldest son of Shah 'Alam, and for Muhammad Bedar Bakht Babadur, the son of Sultan Muhammad A'zam Shah *Muhin-pur.* The words *Farzand-zada 'azimu-l kadr* are used for Muhammad 'Azimu-d din, the second son of Shah 'Alam. The expressions *Umdatu-l Mulk Madaru-l Muham* and *an fidwi* are peculiar to Asad Khan, who was honoured with the title of *Amiru-l umara* after the death of Shayista Khan. The term *Khan Firoz Jang* is the abbreviated title of Ghazi'u-d din Khan Firoz Jang. *Nusrat Jang* is the title of Zu-l Fikar Khan. *Mirza Bakshi* is intended for Mirza Sadru-d din Muhammad Khan Safawi. *Mir-atash* for Tarbiyat Khan, and the single word *Hamid* for Hamidu-d din Khan."

The name of the compiler is not mentioned. This *Kalimat-i Taiyibat* has been lithographed at Lucknow in 8 vo., and contains 67 pages, 17 lines to a page. It is in extensive demand.

The *Rakaim-i Karaim* is a somewhat smaller collection, and consists of 48 octavo pages of fifteen lines to a page. It comprises letters written by the Emperor to Mir

'Abdu-l Karim Khan, father of the compiler; and out of compliment to him, the son called the collection by the name of *Rakaim-i Karaim*. The following is extracted from the Preface: "I Saiyid Ashraf Khan Mir Muhammad Husaini do myself the honour of collecting the epistles of the great King 'Alamgir, which were written to my father 'Abdu-l Karim Amir Khan, and of arranging them in the form of a book, which I denominate by the title of *Rakaim-i Karaim*, as that expression is in a manner connected with the name of the late 'Abdu-l Karim. I much regret the loss of most of the Emperor's epistles, which were either despatched to their several addresses without being copied in my father's office, or were destroyed through the ignorance and carelessness of his attendants. However, those which have remained uninjured are most dear to me."

The *Dasturu-l 'Aml Agahi* appears from the following passage in the Introduction to have been compiled under the orders of Raja Aya Mal. "The dependents of the King 'Alamgir have collected the celebrated epistles from that monarch to the different princes and nobles, into several pamphlets, without arranging them in the form of a regular book; but at the request of Raja Aya Mal, one of his learned servants collected the detached pamphlets into one volume in the Hijra year 1156 (1743 A.D.), and denominated the work *Dasturu-l 'Aml Agahi*. As the style of these epistles was rather difficult to be understood by every one, since the King was very fond of figurative language, the compiler takes the opportunity of giving in this Preface the real meanings of the peculiar expressions used by the King." Then follows the explanation given in the Extract from the *Kalimat-i Taiyibat*.

It appears that another collection had been previously made under the same direction, and that another name is given to that collection. The fourth collection is called *Ramz wa Isharahae 'Alamgir*, and bears the name of the compiler, of which in the case of the *Dasturu-l*

Aml wa Agahi we are left in ignorance. "The correspondence of the Emperor 'Alamgir appears at first sight to consist of ordinary epistles, but in reality they convey the best instruction to kings, and the most useful kind of information to nobles and courtiers. They may be considered harmless friends to all, whether they love retirement or take delight in society. Originally they did not form a regular book, but at the instigation of the celebrated and learned Raja Aya Mal, Budh Mal, surnamed Ram, collected them and formed a book in the year 1151 A.H. (1738 A.D.).

There is another collection bearing the name of *Adab-i 'Alamgiri*. This is composed of letters written by Aurangzeb to his father, sons, and officers. They were collected by *Munshiu-l Mamalik* Shaikh Abu-l Fath, and were arranged and formed into a book by Sadik, entitled *Na-tamam*, a resident of Ambala. The work is noticed in the Catalogue of the Mackenzie Collection (vol. ii. p. 135). [There are several Extracts of this work among Sir H. M. Elliot's MSS., and there is a copy in the British Museum.]

BIBLIOGRAPHICAL NOTICES[1]

TARIKHU-L JANNABI;

AKHBARU-D DAWAL

THE first work, of which the correct name is supposed to be *Bahru-z Zakhkhar*, "the swelling sea," comprises a general history from the beginning of the world to A.H. 997 (A.D. 1589). D'Herbelot quotes the author of the *Kashfu-l Zanun* as saying that this history is called by some *'Ilmu-z Zakhkhar*, "superabundant knowledge," and that it is the most copious history which the Muhammadans have. Haji Khalfa says it has no known title, but that the author of *Akhbaru-d Dawal* mentions it under the name of *Bahr*,

[1] [These are works which Sir M. Elliot had never met with, but about which he has drawn information from other sources.]

and that some learned men call it, *'Ailemu-z Zakhir fi ahwalu-l-awail wau-l-awakhir*, "an overflowing well in the transactions of ancients and moderns."

It gives an account of the creation of the world, the Prophets, Syrians, Sabians, Jews, Christians, the four ancient Persian dynasties, the Kings of the Greeks, of the Israelites, Sultans of Egypt, the Arab tribes, Muhammad, the first four Khalifs, and those of the Ummayide and 'Abbaside dynasties, the Mamluks who ruled over Syria, the several dynasties of the Saffarians, Samanians, Ghorians, Ghaznivides, Dilamites or Buwaibides, Saljukians, Khwarazm-shahis, Changiz Khan, Timur, and their descendants, the Ottoman Emperors, and others.

The work was originally written in Arabic, and translated by the author into Turkish, and abridged by him also in that language. Hence some confusion has arisen in describing it, and a second source of error arises from there being another author of this name, who wrote a history of Timur.

It is divided into 82 sections, each containing a different dynasty; and, although Haji Khalfa notices that several dynasties are omitted which are mentioned in the *Jahan-ara*, yet he states that he knew no work equally copious as a compendium. He therefore abstracted the greater part into his own historical work, entitled *Fazlaka*, but increased the number of the different dynasties to 150. He states also that the *Akhbaru-d Dawal wa asaru-l-awwal*, "the annals of dynasties and the monuments of ancient things," in 380 folios, written A.H. 1008, by Ahmad bin Yusuf bin Ahmad, is an abridgment of Jannabi's history, to which the epitomator adds a little of his own, omitting at the same time many dynasties given by Jannabi.

D'Herbelot varies in giving the name of this author. Under the article "*Gianabi*," he gives it as, Abou Mohammed Mosthafa ben Seid bin Saiyd Hassan al Hosseini, and under "*Turikh al Gianabi*," he calls him, al Gianabi ben Seid Hassan al Roumi. Uri gives his full name as, Abu

Mustafa ben al-Said al-Hasan ben al-Said Senan ben al-Said Ahmed al-Hossini al-Hashemi al-Carshi. He died A.H. 999 (A.D. 1591).

I know of no Manuscript of this work in India, but there was a copy in Sir Gore Ouseley's collection. The name of *Bahru-l Zahhkhar* is familiar, as being the title of a ponderous work devoted to the lives of Muhammadan Saints. It is also the name of the first volume of a modern compilation, called *Majm'au-l Muluk*.

The Arabic history exists at Oxford and St. Petersburg, and the Turkish is in the Royal Library of Vienna. The Bodleian has two copies, both in two volumes ; one copy is in folio, comprising 553 leaves, but there are only 76 sections included in it ; another is in 4to comprising 880 leaves.[3]

TARIKH-I HAJI MUHAMMAD KANDAHARI

THIS work is very frequently quoted by Firishta, both in the General History, as well as in the Histories of Bengal, Sind, and Gujarat, and throughout a period extending from Mahmud of Ghazni to the accession of Akbar. It is, therefore, evidently a General History. The work is also quoted by Ghulam Basit, but probably at second hand.

In the *Sahihu-l Akhbar*, Sarup Chand quotes as one of the authorities to which he is indebted, *Tarikh-i Sadr-i Jahan* by Haji Muhammad Kandahari, in which he has confounded two names together, and rendered himself

---

[3] Compare Uri, *Bibl. Bodl. Codd. MSS. Or.*, pp. 150, 170, 173, Nicoll and Pusey, *ib.* pp. 590, 595 ; Frahn, *Indications Bibliograph.*, No. 221 ; Kœhler, *Eichh, Repert.*, vol. iv. p. 274 ; *Gesch. des Osman. Reiches*, vol. iv. p. 285 ; Haji Khalfa, *Lex. Bibl. et Enc.*, vol. ii. p. 124 ; *Gesch. d. Gold. Horde*, p. xxviii ; *Wien. Jahrb.*, no. lxix. pp. 11, 19 ; *Fundg. d. Or.*, vol. iv. p. 329, vol. vi. p. 370 ; Fleischer's *Cat.*, no. 60 ; *Cat. As. Soc. Beng.*, p. 7 ; *Mod. Univ. Hist.*, vol. I. p. 120, vol. ix. p. 320 ; Gemaldesaal, *Pref.*, p. xl.

open to the suspicion of quoting works which he never saw,—a practice by no means uncommon with our modern historiographers.

I cannot learn that there is any copy of this work extant.

• (See Briggs's *Firishta*, vol. i. pp. 52, 408, vol. iv. pp. 48, 345, 401).

FUTUHU-S SALATIN

The "Victories of the Sultans" would seem, if we may judge by the title, to be a General History. It is quoted in the preface of the *Tabakat-i Akbari* as one of the authorities on which that history is founded.

Firishta, under the reign of Ghiyasu-d din Tughlik, quotes this anecdote from it.

"As the King was near the hills of Tirhut, the Raja appeared in arms, but was pursued into the woods. Finding his army could not penetrate them, the King alighted from his horse, called for a hatchet, and cut down one of the trees with his own hand. The troops, on seeing this, applied themselves to work with such spirit, that the forest seemed to vanish before them. They arrived at length at the fort, surrounded by seven ditches full of water, and defended by a high wall. The King invested the place, filled up the ditches, and destroyed the wall in three weeks. The Raja and his family were taken, and great booty was obtained, and the Government of Tirhut was conferred upon Ahmad Khan."

Briggs observes in a note, "I understand this is a compilation of little authority, and may be ranked with the *Jami'u-l Hikayat*, or other collections of historical romances."

TARIKH-I HAKIMAN-I HIND

A HISTORY of India; comprising an Introduction, twelve Sections and Supplement.

Introduction.—The sovereigns of India, from Shem, the son of Noah, to Anand Deo.

1st Sect.—The Sultans of Lahore, from Nasiru-d din Subuktigin, to Khusru, son of Khusru Shah. 2nd Sect.—Kings of Dehli, from Mu'izzu-d din Muhammad Sam to Akbar. 3rd Sect.—Kings of the Dakhin in six Chapters, treating of the Kings of Kulbarga, Bijapur, Ahmadnagar, Telingana, Birar and Bidar. 4th Sect.—Princes of Gujarat. 5th Sect.—Princes of Malwa. 6th Sect.—Princes of Burhanpur. 7th Sect.—Kings of Bengal. 8th Sect.—Kings of Sind and Tatta. 9th Sect.—Princes of Multan. 10th Sect.—Kings of Kashmir. 11th Sect.—Rulers of Malabar. 12th Sect.—The holy men of Hindustan. Supplement.—A description of Hindustan.

Author unknown; the work follows the same order, and so would appear to be an abridgment of Firishta.[1]

TARKH-I HAIDAR RAZ

THIS is a very good general history of the world, which was begun in 1611 A.D., and took the compiler twenty years to complete. The author was a native of Eastern Persia, and a contemporary of Firishta. He avows that he is a mere copyist, even of the words of his authorities, and states that the chief source of his History of Hindustan is the *Tarikh-i Alfi*, from which he has extracted no less than sixty thousand lines. Wilken, who makes great use of this author in his notes to his translation of the History of the Ghaznivide Emperors, says that the first volume alone of this work, which is in the Royal Library of Berlin, comprises no less than 737 leaves, and even this is not perfect. I have never heard of the work in India, but it is quoted under the name of *Tarikh-i Mirza Haidar*, by Nizamu-d

---

[1] *Mackenzie Collection*, vol. ii. p. 126.

din Ahmad Bakhshi,[1] as one of the chief sources of his information.[2]

KASAID OF BADR CHACH.

[THE author of these Odes, whose real name was Badru-d din, "the full moon of religion," was more familiarly known as Badr-i Chach, from his native country of Chach, or Tashkand. He came to India and attracted some notice at the Court of Muhammad Tughlik, as may be gathered from the following extracts of his poems. His *Kasaid*, or Odes, were lithographed at Lucknow in 1845, and there is a short notice of them in Stewart's Catalogue of Tippoo's Library, and in Sprenger's Catalogue of the Oude Libraries, p. 367. Beyond this, nothing is known of him. The following extracts and notes are entirely the work of Sir H. Elliot.]

Congratulations on the Arrival of a Khila't from the 'Abbasi Khalifa

Gabriel, from the firmament of Heaven, has proclaimed the glad tidings, that a robe of honour and Patent have reached the Sultan from the Khalifa, just as the verses of the Kuran honoured Muhammad by their arrival from the Court of the immortal God. * * * The Imam has given the Shah absolute power over all the world, and this intelligence has reached all other Shahs throughout the seven climates. The Patent of the other sovereigns of the world has been revoked, for an autograph grant has been despatched from the eternal Capital. The wells of the envious have become as dry as that of Joseph, now that the Egyptian robe has been received in Hindustan from Canaan. * * * A veritable *'Id* has arrived to the Faithful, now that twice in one year a *khila't* has reached the

---

[1] This cannot be the same work, for Nizam Ahmad's work does not come down later than 1592.
[2] *Journ. As.* 1851, p. 147; *Jahrbucher*, no. 73, p. 25; Frœhn, no. 218; *Goldene Horde*, p. xxiv.

Sultan from the *Amiru-l Muminin*. * * * Rajab arrived here on his return in the month of Muharram, 746 H.[1] (May, 1345 A.D.). * * * The king now never mentions his desire of sitting on an ivory throne, since his enemies sit on the point of elephants' tusks.[2] * * * Be happy, oh Badr, for by the grace of God, and liberality of the king, your difficulties have ceased, and the period of benefactions has arrived.

Decorations of Dehli upon the same occasion

Yesternight, at the time that the sun, the king with the golden garments, invested itself with a black mantle, and the king of the host of darkness,[3] whose name is the moon, filled the emerald vault with sparks of gold, a robe of honour and a patent of sovereignty arrived, for the king of sea and land, from the lord Khalifa, the saint of his time, Ahmad 'Abbas, the Imam of God, the heir of the prophet of mankind. An order went forth that the embroiderers of curtains should prepare a beautiful and

---

[1] This is a very difficult passage, and variously interpreted. I have made as much sense of it as it seems capable of bearing. The literal translation is: "On the very date on which one month was in excess of the year 700 from this journey, in the month of Muharram, the before Sha'ban arrived." The chronogrammatic value of "one month" is forty-six; some copies, by the omission of the *alif*, make it "forty-five," and some only "nine," which latter is out of the question. Rajab is the month before Sha'ban, and that is also the name of the ambassador who had been sent by Muhammad Tughlik to the Khalifa. Firishta says one *khila't* arrived in 744 H., and another in 747 H. Here a contemporary says the second arrived in 746 H., or it may be 745 H., and that both *khila't*s arrived within one year. The introduction of the Khalifa's name upon Muhammad Tughlik's coins begins as early as 741 H.; but this must have occurred before the arrival of an ambassador, and sufficiently accounts for the errors in the name of the reigning Khalifa, which do not occur at a period subsequent to this embassy. See T. Thomas, *Coins of the Patan Sultans*, New Edition, pp. 254, 259, and Frachn, Recensio, p. 177.

[2] That is, your enemies are placed before elephants, to be gored or trampled to death by elephants.

[3] There is a double meaning here—the "host of darkness" being, in the original, "the army of Hind;" and the "black mantle," "the *khila't* of the 'Abbasis;" which image also occurs in the preceding ode.

costly pavilion in the centre of four triumphal arches, which were so lofty that the vault of heaven appeared in comparison like a green fly. Each arch was adorned with golden vestments, like a bride. The floors were spread with beautiful carpets, and there were ponds of water to excite the envy of Kansar, the rivulet of paradise. In the chambers poets recited verses; songsters, like Venus, sang in each balcony. The chamberlains were in attendance, with their embroidered sleeves; the judges, with their turbans; the princes, with their waistbands. All classes of the people assembled round the buildings to witness the scene. This gay assemblage had collected because a *khila't* and Patent had been sent by the lord Imam. The contents of it were : "May everything on the face of the earth, in the fire and in the water, remain under the protection of the king—Turk, Rum, Khurasan, Chin, and Sham—both that which is good, and that which is bad ! If an azure canopy be granted, the heaven is at his command ; if a red crown be desired, the sun will provide it. Let his titles be proclaimed from every pulpit—the Sultan of East and West, the King of Kings by sea and land, the Defender of the Faith, Muhammad Tughlik, the Just, in dignity like Saturn, in splendour like the Messiah !" The Imam has sent a *khila't* black as the apple of the eye, calculated to spread the light of the law through the hearts of men. For fear of the justice of thy government, the hart and the lion consort in the forest. May the eyes of thy enemies shed tears of blood. May he who raises his head against thy authority, have his face blackened, and his tongue slit, like a pen-reed; and so long as the moon is sometimes round as a shield, and sometimes bent like a bow, may arrows pierce the heart of thy ruthless enemies. May every success attend Badr through thy good fortune, and may he never be visited by any calamities of the time !

In Celebration of a Festival

Doubtless, this festival appears as if it were held in Paradisc, in which armies of angels stand on the right and left. A thousand crowned heads are bowed in reverence; a thousand throned warriors stand awaiting orders; a thousand stars (armies) are there, and under each star are arranged a thousand banners. In each course behind the screens are a thousand songsters, melodious as nightingales. If the palace of a thousand pillars were not like Paradise, why should rewards and punishments be distributed there like as on the day of judgment? Certainly this abode of happiness, Khurramabad, is chosen as a royal residence, because there the king, by his execution of the laws, acknowledges his subservience to the Khalifa of the world, Abu-l Rabi' Sulaiman, the celebrated Imam, to whom the Khusru of Hind is a servant and slave in body, heart, and soul. This Khusru is a holy warrior, Muhammad Tughlik, at whose gate the King of Chin and Khitn is in waiting, like a Hindu porter. * * * The blade of thy sword smites the necks of thy enemies, and with equal power does thy hand wield the pen, clothed in a yellow tunic, like a Hindu.

* * * * *

On the Capture of Nagarkot

When the sun was in Cancer, the king of the time took the stone fort of Nagarkot, in the year 758 H. (1357 A.D.). * * * It is placed between rivers, like the pupil of an eye, and the fortress has so preserved its honour, and is so impregnable, that neither Sikandar nor Dara were able to take it. Within are the masters of the mangonels; within also are beauties resplendent as the sun. Its chiefs are all strong as buffalos, with necks like a rhinoceros. Its inhabitants are all travelling on the high road to hell and perdition, and are *ghuls*, resembling dragons. The exalted king of the kings of the earth arrived at night at this fortress, with 100,000 champions. His army contained 1,000 stars, and under each star 1,000 banners were displayed. * * * Muhammad Tughlik is obedient to the laws of Muhammad, the apostle, and the orders of his vicegerent, Abu-l Rabi' Sulaiman Mustakfi, the essence of the religion of the prophet, the light of the family of Khalifas, the Imam of God, to whom the king is a servant and slave in body, heart, and soul.

· · · · ·

The Author is despatched to Deogir

On the 1st of Sha'ban, in the year 745, represented by the letters in "The power of the king," orders were issued that I should go to the country of Deogir, and I was thus addressed: "Oh, Badr, accompanied by Jamal Malik, the poet, and Nekroz, the slave, take thy departure with a pomp worthy of Rustam. May he who accomplishes all designs aid thee; may the God of both worlds protect thee; but speak not of Deogir, for it is Daulatabad to which I allude, a fort exalted to the heavens! Although it is but a point in my kingdom, it comprises what is equal to 1,000 kingdoms of Jamshid. * * * Go to the court of the governor of the country, Katlagh Khan, and acquire honour by this presentation, and having thy mouth in honey, say thus from me: 'Oh thou, from whose lips sugar distils, in whose fortunate[a] breast the light of the flame of the knowledge of God is reflected; thou, that art the best of those possessed of gold; thou, that art the essence of those who are excellent among men; thou, whose bounteous hand is so munificent that the fathomless ocean is but a drop compared with it; come, and gratify me by your arrival, as water does the thirsty. If thou hast any desire to reach the summit of thy exaltation, proceed towards the north.[b] Come and feast thy eyes upon the black *khila't*, so propitiously sent by the Imam of the time, and look with due reverence on the Patent which has issued from the Khalifa Abu-l 'Abbas Ahmad, the sun of the earth, and the shadow of

---

[a] *Mubarak* is the Persian translation of *Katlagh*.
[b] The annotator says, "Proceed on a mission to the Khalifa;" but this is a very imperfect interpretation.

God. It is through his justice that an antelope is able to seize the tail of a wolf. Use every exertion to come to the royal court, for henceforward you and I have obtained everlasting salvation.'

"When thou, oh Badr, hast delivered this address to the Khan, kiss his hands and bow down, like a pen dipping into an inkstand. Obey every order that he gives, and deem yourself honoured with every gift that he presents. * * * When the equipage of Jalalat Khan proceeds in state to the throne of the Sultan, the king of earth and sea, proclaim to the world that the Khwaja is coming, like the resplendent sun, with 100,000 footmen, 100,000 horsemen, 100,000 spears, and 100,000 bows, sitting in his silver *ambari*, like the moon in the milky way."

● ● ● ● ●

In Commemoration of the Building of Khurramabad

● ● ● ● ●

The inscriptions over its gateway record, in verse, the praise of the Khalifa repeatedly; may his throne be established to eternity, as well as that of the King of the World, who has declared that it is his pleasure to serve the Imam of God. The Shah has given it the name of Khurramabad, and Zahiru-l Jaiush was its architect, the slave of the lord of the universe, the prelate of religion, the most select among the pious. This fortunate building was completed in Muharram, in the year 744 H. (June, 1343 A.D.). Badr has strung the pearl of this ode in one night and made it worthy of ornamenting the ears of the nobles of the land.

On the same subject

● ● ● ● ●

Without, though the courts, full of armies, are raising a tumult and uproar, yet within it is so quiet, that prayers for pardon can be offered up.* * * * All is so still and clear that the ear of man might hear the humming of a fly's wing reverberate like music. * * * Speak not of a fort, speak not of a sarai, for in appearance and stability it is like the Ka'bah of Paradise. Zahiru-d din erected this blessed structure by the propitious order of the Khusru of the time, the director of the architects, and in the name of the Khalifa. May his life be prolonged for the confirmation of the religion of Muhammad, the Apostle of God. It was completed on the date, "Enter thou into Paradise," or, that I may explain more openly, 744 H. I have been entitled by the king, Fakhru-z zaman; call me not by that name, but rather the sweet-noted parrot.

In Celebration of the Completion of the Shah-nama

In the year of Arabia, represented by "the power of the king" (745 H., 1344 A.D.), heaven completed the verses which I had strung together. Every line was like a pearl, which dazzled the eye in the dead of night. * * * The whole of the poem is filled with praises of the king, Shah Muhammad, the defender of the law of the Prophet, and by right the ruler of the earth, by order of the Imam. Everywhere crowned heads swear fealty to him, everywhere celebrated men are the slaves of his behests.

* * * * *

MASALIKU-L ABSAR FI MAMALIKU-L AMSAR
OF
SHAHABU-D DIN ABU-L 'ABBAS AHMAD

["Travels of the Eyes into the Kingdoms of Different Countries." This is the work of Shahabu-d din 'Abu-l 'Abbas Ahmad, also called 'Umari and Dimashki, or

---

* In allusion to the mode in which these multi-columned buildings are constructed, so as to render the centre compartments private, while externally all appears exposed.

native of Damascus. He was born in the year 697 H. (1297 A.D.), and died at Damascus in 749 (1348 A.D.). Shahabu-d din says little about himself and his family, but he mentions that his ancestors were, like himself, employed in the service of the Sultan of Egypt. His father, Kazi Mohiu-d din, was secretary of secret despatches at Damascus, and after being dismissed from that office, and remaining some time without employ, became chief of the department of secret correspondence in Egypt. Shahabu-d din assisted his father in both his offices, but he incurred disgrace, and retired into private life at Damascus, and so lived until his death.

Shahabu-d din was a man of very considerable learning and ability. He studied different sciences under men of celebrity, and his extensive works testify to his learning, research, and literary activity. He is known to have written seven different works, inclusive of the one now under notice. Most of his writings have perished, or are at least unknown, but the *Masalik*, which is the most important of them in its extent and research, has come down to us in an imperfect state. The complete work consisted of twenty volumes, but of these only five are known to be extant. They are in the Bibliotheque Imperiale at Paris, and in 1938 M. Quatremere published in Tome XIII. of the *Notices et Extraits des MSS*, his description and specimens of the work, from which the present notice and the following extracts have been taken by the Editor. So early as 1758 Deguignes gave a short notice of the MS. in the *Journal des Savants*, and he frequently refers to the author under the surname of *Marakashi* in his *Histoire des Huns*; but M. Quatremere shows this title of *Marakashi*, or "native of Morocco," to be a mistake.

The MS. is a small folio of 231 leaves, and consists of six chapters. 1. Description of Hind and Sind. 2. The Empire and family of Changiz Khan. 3. The Kingdom of Jilan. 4. The Kurds, Lurs, and other mountain tribes. 5. Turk states in Asia Minor, with notices of the empires of Trebizond and Constantinople. 6. Egypt, Syria, and Hijjaz.

At the close of his notices of India, he mentions the name of Muhammad Tughlik as the reigning sovereign, and the general tenor of his observations points unmistakably to that able but perverse ruler. The author quotes occasionally the works of other authors on geography and history, and among them Abu-l Fida and Juwaini ; but he depends principally on the oral information supplied by intelligent and learned travellers with whom he had come in contact. His method of gathering and using information is apparent in the following extracts. The work stood high in Oriental estimation, and was often quoted by later writers—among others by the author of the *Nuzhatu-l Kulub*.]

EXTRACTS

India is a most important country, with which no other country in the world can be compared in respect of extent, riches, the numbers of its armies, the pomp and splendour displayed by the sovereign in his progresses and habitations, and the power of the empire. * * * The inhabitants are remarkable for their wisdom and great intelligence ; no people are better able to restrain their passions, nor more willing to sacrifice their lives, for what they consider agreeable in the sight of God.

According to the information of Siraju-d din Abu-l Fath 'Umar, a lawyer, and a native of the province of Oudh, who had lived long at the court of the Sultan of Dehli, the dominions of that monarch consisted of twenty-three principal provinces. 1. Dehli. 2. Dawakir (Deogir). 3. Multan. 4. Kahran (Kuhram). 5. Samana. 6. Siwistan. 7. Uch. 8. Hasi (Hansi). 9. Sarsuti (Sirsah). 10. Ma'bar. 11. Tilank (Telingana). 12. Gujarat. 13. Badaun. 14. Oudh. 15. Kanauj. 16. Lakhnauti. 17. Bihar. 18. Karra. 19. Malwa. 20. Lahor. 21. Kalanor (Gwalior ?). 22. Jajnagar. 23. Tilanj Darusamand (Telingana (?) and Dwarasamudra).

According to the account of Shaikh Mubarak, the city of Dehli is the capital of the kingdom of India. Next comes *Dawakir* (Deogir), which was founded by the Sultan of that empire, and named by him "*Kabbatu-l Islam, or the Metropolis of Islam.*" This place, said the Shaikh, is situated in the third climate. When I left it six years ago the buildings were not completed, and I doubt if they are yet finished, the extent it covers being so great, and the number of its intended edifices so vast. The king divided it into quarters, each of them intended for men of the same profession. Thus there was the quarter of the troops, that of the ministers and clerks, that of the *kazis* and learned men, that of the *shaikhs* and *fakirs*, and that of the merchants and those who carry on trades. Each quarter was to contain within it everything necessary for its wants, mosques, minarets, markets, baths, mills, ovens, and workmen of every trade, including even blacksmiths, dyers, and curriers, so that the inhabitants should have no necessity to resort elsewhere for buying or selling, or the other requirements of life. Each quarter was to form a separate town, entirely independent of those surrounding it.

•   •   •   •   •

I questioned the Shaikh Mubarak about the city of Dehli and the court of its sovereign, and I obtained from him the following details. "Dehli consists of several cities which have become united, and each of which has a name of its own. Dehli, which was one among them, has given its name to all the rest. It is both long and broad, and covers a space of about forty miles in circumference. The houses are built of stone and brick, and the roofs of wood. The floors are paved with a white stone, like marble. None of the houses are more than two stories high, and some only one. It is only in the palace of the Sultan that marble is used for pavement. But if I can believe the Shaikh Abu Bakr bin Khallal, this description applies only to the old houses of Dehli, for the new ones are built differently. According to the same informant, Dehli comprises an aggregate of twenty-one cities. Gardens extend on three sides of it, in a straight line for twelve thousand paces. The western side is not so furnished, because it borders on a mountain. Dehli contains a thousand colleges, one of which belongs to the *Shafa'is*, the rest to the *Hanafis*. In it there are about seventy hospitals, called *Daru-sh Shifa*, or houses of cure. In the city, and those dependent upon it, the chapels and hermitages amount to 2,000. There are great monasteries, large open spaces, and numerous baths. The water used by the people is drawn from wells of little depth, seldom exceeding seven cubits. Hydraulic wheels are placed at their tops. The people drink rain-water, which is collected in large reservoirs constructed for that purpose, the distance across each of them being a bowshot, or even more. The chief mosque is celebrated for its minaret, which, in point of altitude, is said to have no equal in the world. If the statement of Shaikh Burhanu-d din Bursi can be believed, the height of this part of the edifice is 600 cubits.

According to Shaikh Mubarak, the palaces of the Sultan of Dehli are exclusively occupied by the Sultan, his wives, concubines, eunuchs, male and female slaves, and *mamluks*. None of the *khans* and *amirs* are permitted to dwell there. They make their appearance there only when they come to wait upon the Sultan, which they do twice a day, morning and afternoon. Afterwards, each one of them retires to his own house.

As regards the great officers of State, those of the highest rank are called *khans*, then the *maliks*,[1] then the *amirs*, then the *sifahsalars* (generals), and, lastly, the officers (*jand*). The court of the sovereign comprises eighty *khans*, or even more. The army consists of 9,00,000 horsemen, some of whom are stationed near the

---

[1] The French translation says "rois," but I have no hesitation in substituting "*malik*," which is no doubt the original word.

prince, and the rest are distributed in the various provinces of the empire. All are inscribed in the registers of the State, and partake of the liberality of their sovereign. These troops consist of Turks, inhabitants of Khata, Persians, and Indians. Among them are to be found *athletæ (pahlawan)*, runners, *(shattar)*, and men of every kind. They have excellent horses, magnificent armour, and a fine costume. * * * The Sultan has 3,000 elephants, which, when accoutred for battle, wear a covering of iron gilded. * * * He has 20,000 Turk *mamluks.* * * * It is not the same in India as in Egypt and Syria, where the *maliks, amirs,* and generals have in their service men whom they maintain out of their own resources. In India the officer has only to care for himself. As to the soldiers, the Sultan summons them for service, and they are paid from the public treasury. The sums granted to a *khan,* a *malik,* an *amir,* or a general, are given exclusively for his own personal maintenance. The chamberlains and other dignitaries; the military men, such as the *khans,* the *maliks,* and the *amirs,* all have a rank in proportion to the importance of their employ. The *isfah-salars* (generals) have no right to approach the Sultan. It is from this class that governors and other similar functionaries are chosen. The *khan* has 10,000 horse under his command, the *malik,* 1,000; the *amir,* 100; and the *isfah-salar* a smaller number. The *khans, maliks, amirs,* and *isfah-salars* receive the revenues of places assigned to them by the treasury, and if these do not increase, they never diminish. Generally speaking, they bring in much more than their estimated value. The *khan* receives a grant of two *lacs* of *tankas,* each *tanka* being worth eight *dirhams.* This sum belongs to him personally, and he is not expected to disburse any part of it to the soldiers who fight under his orders. The *malik* receives an amount varying from 60,000 to 50,000 *tankas,* the *amir* from 40,000 to 30,000, and the *isfah-salar* 20,000, or thereabouts. The pay of the officer varies from 10,000 to 1,000 *tankas.* A *mamluk* receives 500 *tankas,* and all receive, in addition, food and raiment, and forage for their horses. Soldiers and *mamluks* do not receive grants of land-revenue, but draw their pay in money from the public treasury. The officers have villages of which they receive the revenues. As this same traveller observed to me, the revenues of these lands, if they do not increase, certainly do not decrease. Some of the officers receive double, and even more than that, in excess of the estimated value of their grants.

The slaves of the Sultan each receive a monthly allowance for their maintenance of two *mans* of wheat and rice, and a daily allowance of three *sirs* of meat, with all the necessary accompaniments. Besides, he receives ten *tankas* per month, and four suits of clothes every year.

The Sultan has a manufactory, in which 400 silk-weavers are employed, and where they make stuffs of all kinds for the dresses of persons attached to the Court, for robes of honour and presents, in addition to the stuffs which are brought every year from China, 'Irak, and Alexandria. Every year the Sultan distributes 200,000 complete dresses; 100,000 in spring, and 100,000 in autumn. The spring dresses consist principally of the goods manufactured at Alexandria. Those of the autumn are almost exclusively of silk manufactured at Dehli or imported from China and 'Irak. Dresses are also distributed to the monasteries and hermitages.

The Sultan keeps in his service 500 manufacturers of golden tissues, who weave the gold brocades worn by the wives of the Sultan, and given away as presents to the *amirs* and their wives. Every year he gives away 10,000 Arab horses, of excellent breed, sometimes with saddle and bridle, sometimes without. * * * As to the hacks which the Sultan distributes every year, their number is incalculable. He gives them in lots or by hundreds. Notwithstanding the number of horses in India, and notwithstanding the numbers annually imported, the Sultan has horses brought from all countries, and buys them at high prices for presents. These animals are consequently always dear, and yield a good profit to the horse-dealers.

The Sultan has under him a *naib*, chosen from among the *khans*, who bears the title of *Amriya*, and enjoys, as his official appanage, a considerable province, as large as 'Irak. He also has a *wazir*, who has a similar large appanage. This officer has four deputies called *shak*, who receive 20,000 to 40,000 *tankas* per annum. He has four *dabirs*, or secretaries, each of whom receives the revenue of a large maritime town. Each of them has under his orders about 800 clerks, the lowest and worst paid of whom receives 10,000 *tankas* a year. Some of the highest rank have towns and villages, and some have both (pay and lands) to the value of fifty (thousand).

The *Sadr-i Jahan*, or *Kaziu-l kuzat*, which office is held, at the time I am writing, by Kamalu-d din, son of Burhanu-d din, has ten towns, producing a revenue of about 60,000 *tankas*. This dignitary is also called *Sadru-l Islam*, and is the chief officer of justice. The *Shaikhu-l Islam*, who corresponds to our *Shaikhu-sh shuyukh*, has the same revenue. The *Muhtasib*, or chief of the police, has a village which brings him in about 800 *tankas*.

At the Court of this prince there are 1,200 physicians, 10,000 falconers, who ride on horseback, and carry the birds trained for hawking, 800 beaters to go in front and put up the game, 3,000 dealers, who sell the articles required for hawking, 500 table companions, 1,200 musicians, not including the *mamluk* musicians to the number of 1,000, who are more especially charged with the teaching of music, and 1,000 poets skilled in one of three languages, Arabic, Persian, or Indian. All these are men of fine taste, who are included in the establishment of the Court, and receive magnificent presents. If the Sultan hears that one of his musicians has sung before any other person, he has him put to death. I asked my informant what pay these various officers received, but he did not know; he could only inform me that the table companions of the prince held some of them one, and some of them two towns; and that each of them, according to his rank, received 40,000, 30,000, or 20,000 *tankas*, without taking into account dresses, robes of honour, and other presents.

According to Shaikh Mubarak, the Sultan gives two audiences daily, in the morning and in the evening, and a repast is then served, at which 20,000 men are present, *khans, maliks, amirs, isfah-salars,* and the principal officers. At his private meals, that is, at his dinner and supper, the Sultan receives learned lawyers to the number of 200, who eat with him and converse upon learned matters. Shaikh Abu Bakr bin Khallal Bazzi told me that he asked the Sultan's cook how many animals were killed daily to supply the royal table, and the reply was 2,500 oxen, 2,000 sheep, without taking into account fatted horses and birds of all descriptions. * * *

The *amriya* has under his charge the army and the people at large. Lawyers and learned men, whether inhabitants of the country or foreigners, are under the inspection of the *Sadr-i Jahan*. The *fakirs*, whether natives or strangers, are under the *Shaikhu-l Islam*. Lastly, all travellers, ambassadors, or others, men of letters, poets, both native and foreign, are all under the *dabirs*, or secretaries. * * *

When the Sultan goes hunting his suite is less numerous. He only takes with him 100,000 horsemen and 200 elephants. Four wooden houses of two stories are carried in his train by 200 camels. Tents and pavilions of all kinds follow. When he travels from one place to another, for pleasure or for other motives, he takes with him 30,000 horsemen, 200 elephants, and 1,000 led horses, with saddles and bridles worked with gold, and with other trappings of gold, set with pearls and jewels.

The Sultan is generous and liberal, and at the same time full of humility. Abu-s Safa 'Umar bin Ishak Shabali informed me that he saw this monarch at the funeral of a *fakir* of great sanctity, and that he bore the coffin on his shoulders. He is noted for knowing the Holy Book by heart, as also the law book called *Hidaya*, which expounds the principles of the school of Abu Hanifa. He excels in all intellectual accomplishments. He possesses in the very highest degree a talent for caligraphy. He is given to religious exercises, and is careful to regulate his passions. To these advantages he adds literary acquirements. He is fond of reciting verses, composing them, and hearing them read, when he readily seizes their most hidden allusions. He likes to consult with learned men, and to converse with men of merit. He is also particularly fond of contending with poets in Persian, a language which he knows perfectly, and understands all its niceties of expression. * * *

The stories I have been told of the benevolence and generosity of this Sultan towards strangers, and to all who have recourse to him, pass all belief. * * *

The Sultan never ceases to show the greatest zeal in making war upon the infidels, both by sea and land. * * * Every day thousands of slaves are sold at a very low price, so great is the number of prisoners. According to the unanimous statements of the travellers I have cited, the value, at Dehli, of a young slave girl, for domestic service, does not exceed eight *tankas*. Those who are deemed fit to fill the parts of domestic and concubine sell for about fifteen *tankas*. In other cities the prices are still lower. Abu-s Safa 'Umar bin Ishak Shabali assured me that he bought a young slave in the flower of his youth for four *dirhams*. The rest may be understood from this. But still, in spite of the low price of slaves, 200,000 *tankas*, and even more, are paid for young Indian girls. I inquired the reason, * * * and was told that these young girls are remarkable for their beauty, and the grace of their manners. * * *

According to what I heard from Shabali, the smallest quantity of wine is not to be found either in shops or in private houses : so great is the Sultan's aversion to it and so severe the punishments with which he visits its votaries. Besides, the inhabitants of India have little taste for wine and intoxicating drinks, but content themselves with betel, an agreeable drug, the use of which is permitted without the slightest objection. * * *

From the information of the learned Siraju-d din Abu-s Safa 'Umar Shabali, it appears that the Sultan is very anxious to know all that passes in his territories, and to understand the position of all those who surround him, whether civilians or soldiers. He has emissaries, called intelligencers, who are divided into a great number of classes. One goes among the soldiers and people. When any fact comes under his notice which ought to be communicated to the Sultan, he reports it to the officer above him; this one, in like manner, communicates it to his superior; and so in due course the fact comes to the knowledge of the Sultan. For communicating the events which happen in distant provinces, there are established, between the capital and the chief cities of the different countries, posts, placed at certain distances from each other, which are like the post-relays in Egypt and Syria; but they are less wide apart, because the distance between them is not more than four bow-shots, or even less. At each of these posts ten swift runners are stationed, whose duty it is to convey letters to the next station without the least delay. As soon as one of these men receives a letter, he runs off as rapidly as possible, and delivers it to the next runner, who starts immediately with similar speed, while the former returns quietly to his own post. Thus a letter from a very distant place is conveyed in a very short time with greater celerity than if it had been transmitted by post, or by camel express. At each of these post-stations there are mosques, where prayers are said, and where travellers can find shelter, reservoirs full of good water, and markets where all things necessary for the food of man and beast can be purchased, so that there is very little necessity for carrying water, or food, or tents.

All through the country which separates the two capitals of the empire, Dehli and Deogir, the Sultan has had drums placed at every post-station. When any event occurs in a city, or when the gate of one is opened or closed, the drum is instantly beaten. The next nearest drum is then beaten, and in this manner the Sultan is daily and exactly informed at what time the gates of the most distant cities are opened or closed. * * *

I will now speak about the money, and afterwards about the price of provisions, seeing that these are regulated and calculated upon the value of money. Shaikh Mubarak informed me that the *red lac* consists of 100,000 *tankas* (of gold), and the *white lac* of 100,000 *tankas* (of silver). The gold *tanka*, called the *red tanka*, is equal to three *miskals* and the silver *tanka* comprises eight *dirhams hashtkani*.² The *dirham hashtkani* has the same weight as the silver *dirham* current in Egypt and Syria. The value of both is the same, with scarcely the slightest difference. The *dirham hashtkani* answers to four *dirhams sultanis*, otherwise called *dukanis*. A *dirham sultani* is worth the third of a *dirham shashkani*, which is a third kind of silver coin current in India, and which is worth three-fourths of the *dirham hashtkani*. A piece, which is the half of the *dirham sultani*, is called *yakani* (piece of one), and is worth one *jital*. Another *dirham*, called *dwazdahkani* (piece of twelve), passes for a *hashtkani* and a half. Another coin, called *shanzdahkani*, corresponds to two *dirhams*. So the silver coins current in India are six, i.e. the *dirham shanzdahkani*, the *dwazdahkani*, the *hashtkani*, the *shashkani*, the *sultani*, and the *yakani*. The least of these pieces is the *dirham sultani*. These three kinds of *dirhams* are employed in commerce, and are taken universally, but there is no one of more general use than the *dirham sultani*, which is worth

---

² I retain the original spelling, as Thomas contends that *kani*, and not *gani*, is the true reading. As, however, the Arabic has no *g*, but uses *k* for it, this passage decides nothing. See *supra*.

a quarter of the *dirham* of Egypt and of Syria. The *dirham sultani* is equal to eight *fals* [or *fulus*]; the *jital* to four *fals;* and the *dirham hashtkani*, which corresponds exactly to the silver *dirham* of Egypt and Syria, is worth thirty-two *fals*.

The *ritl* of India, which is called *sir*, weighs seventy *miskals*, which, estimated in *dirhams* of Egypt, is worth 102⅔. Forty *sirs* make one *man*. They do not know the way of measuring grain in India.

As to the price of provisions, wheat, which is the dearest article, sells for a *dirham hashtkani* and a half the *man*. Barley costs one *dirham* the *man*. Rice, one *dirham* three-quarters the *man;* but some sorts of this grain are higher in price. Two *mans* of peas cost a *dirham hashtkani*. Beef and goats' flesh are of the same price, and are sold at the rate of six *sirs* for a *dirham sultani*, which is the quarter of a *dirham hashtkani*. Mutton sells at four *sirs* the *dirham sultani*. A goose costs two *dirham hashtkanis*, and four fowls can be bought for one *hashtkani*. Sugar sells at five *sirs* the *hashtkani*, and sugar-candy at four *sirs* the *dirham*. A well-fatted sheep of the first quality sells for a *tanka*, which represents eight *dirhams hashtkanis*. A good ox sells for two *tankas*, and sometimes for less. Buffaloes at the same price. The general food of the Indians is beef and goats' flesh. I asked Shaikh Mubarak if this usage arose from the scarcity of sheep, and he replied that it was a mere matter of habit, for in all the villages of India there are sheep in thousands. For a *dirham* of the money of Egypt four fowls can be bought of the best quality. Pigeons, sparrows, and other birds are sold very cheap. All kinds of game, birds, and quadrupeds, are extremely plentiful. There are elephants and rhinoceroses, but the elephants of the country of the Zinjes are the most remarkable. * * *

Our *shaikh*, the marvel of the age, Shamsu-d din Isfabani, gave me the following details. Kutbu-d din

Shirazi maintained that alchemy was a positive science. One day I argued with him, and endeavoured to prove the falsity of the art. He replied, "You know very well the quantity of gold that is annually consumed in the fabrication of various articles and objects of many kinds. The mines are far from producing a quantity equal to that which is thus withdrawn. As regards India, I have calculated that for the last three thousand years that country has not exported gold into other countries, and whatever has entered it has never come out again. Merchants of all countries never cease to carry pure gold into India, and to bring back in exchange commodities of herbs and gums. If gold were not produced in an artificial way, it would altogether have disappeared." Our *shaikh*, Shahabu-d din, observed upon this that what this author asserted of gold going into India, and never coming out again, was perfectly true; but the conclusion which he drew from this fact, as to alchemy being a real science, was false and illusory.

He adds the following statement : "I have heard say that one of the predecessors of the Sultan, after making great conquests, carried off from the countries he had subdued as much gold as required 13,000 oxen to carry."

I must add, that the inhabitants of India have the character of liking to make money and hoard it. If one of them is asked how much property he has, he replies, "I don't know, but I am the second or third of my family who has laboured to increase the treasure which an ancestor deposited in a certain cavern, or in certain holes, and I do not know how much it amounts to." The Indians are accustomed to dig pits for the reception of their hoards. Some form an excavation in their houses like a cistern, which they close with care, leaving only the opening necessary for introducing the gold pieces. Thus they accumulate their riches. They will not take worked gold, either broken or in ingots, but in their fear of fraud refuse all but coined money.

The following information I derived from the Shaikh Burhanu-d din Abu Bakr bin Khallah Muhammad Barzi, the Sufi. The Sultan [Muhammad Tughlik] sent an army against a country bordering upon Deogir, at the extremity of that province. It is inhabited by infidels, and all its princes bear the title of ra [rai]. The reigning prince, finding himself pressed by the troops of the Sultan, made this communication : "Tell your master that if he will leave us at peace, I am ready to send him all the riches he can desire; all he has to do is to send me sufficient beasts to carry the sum he requires." The general sent this proposition to his master, and was ordered to cease hostilities, and to give the rai a safe conduct. When the rai appeared before the Sultan, the latter heaped honours upon him, and said : "I have never heard the like of what you have proposed. What is the amount, then, of those treasures that you undertake to load with gold as many beasts of burden as we like to send ?" The rai replied : "Seven princes have preceded me in the government of my kingdom. Each of them amassed a treasure amounting to seventy *babins*, and all these treasures are still at my disposal." The word *babin*[1] signifies a very large cistern, into which there is a descent by a ladder on each of the four sides. The Sultan, delighted by this statement, ordered his seal to be put on these treasures, which was done. Then he ordered the rai to appoint viceroys in his dominions, and to reside at Dehli. He also invited him to turn Musulman, but on his refusal he allowed him to adhere to his own religion. The rai dwelt at the court of the Sultan, and appointed viceroys to govern his territories. The Sultan assigned him a suitable income, and sent considerable sums into his territories to be distributed as alms among the inhabitants, seeing they were now subjects of the empire. Lastly, he did not touch the *babins*, but left them as they were, under seal.

[1] *Babni* in Hindi signifies a snake's hole, and in Hindu belief snakes keep guard over hidden treasure.

TRAVELS OF IBN BATUTA

Ibn Batuta was a native of Tangiers, who travelled over the greater part of Asia, and visited India in the reign of Muhammad Tughlik. Elphinstone's summary of the character and value of this traveller's writings is so brief and so much to the point that it can hardly be improved. He says Ibn Batuta "could have had no interest in misrepresentation, as he wrote after his return to Africa. He confirms, to the full extent, the native accounts, both of the king's talents and of his crimes, and gives exactly each a picture of mixed magnificence and desolation as one would expect under such a sovereign. 'He found an admirably regulated horse and foot post from the frontiers to the capital, while the country was so disturbed as to make travelling unsafe. He describes Dehli as a most magnificent city, its mosque and walls without an equal on earth; but although the king was then repeopling it, it was almost a desert. 'The greatest city in the world, he said, had the fewest inhabitants.'"

The extracts which follow have been selected as containing the most important and interesting events and facts which he has recorded about India. His details do not always precisely agree with those of the regular historians. He recounted, and no doubt honestly, the information he received from the respectable and well-informed individuals with whom he was brought in contact; and there is an air of veracity about his statements which favourably impresses the reader. In his African home he carefully wrote down that which he had gathered in the free course of conversation. But, while on the one hand he doubtless heard many facts and opinions which the speakers would not have dared to commit to writing and publish, some deduction must be made on the other side for the loose statements and bold assertions which pass current when there is no probability of bringing them to the test of public judgment. Thus he distinctly relates that Muhammad Tughlik compassed the death of his father by an apparent accident, and he is probably right in his statement, but Barni records the catastrophe as a simple accident, and Firishta only notices the charge of foul play to reject and condemn it.

Ibn Batuta was received with much respect at the court of Muhammad Tughlik, and experienced in his own person much of the boundless liberality and some little of the severity of that lavish and savage sovereign. When the traveller arrived in Dehli the king was absent, but the queen-mother received him. He was presented with splendid robes, 2,000 *dinars* in money, and a house to live in. On the return of the Sultan, he was treated yet more splendidly. He received a grant of villages worth 5,000 *dinars* per annum, a present of ten female captives, a fully caparisoned horse from the royal stables, and a further sum of 5,000 *dinars*. Besides this, he was made a judge of Dehli at a salary of 12,000 *dinars* a year, and was allowed to draw the first year in advance. After this he received another present of 12,000 *dinars*, but he records the fact that a deduction of ten per cent. was always made from these presents. He afterwards got into debt to the amount of 45,000 *dinars*, but he presented an Arabic poem to the Sultan in which he recounted his difficulties, and the Sultan undertook to satisfy his creditors. When the sovereign left Dehli he received further marks of his favour and liberality, but subsequently he fell into disgrace for having visited an obnoxious *shaikh*. His account of his terrors is rather amusing. "The Sultan ordered four of his slaves never to lose sight of me in the audience chamber and when such an order is given, it is very rarely that the person escapes. The first day the slaves kept watch over me was a Friday, and the Almighty inspired me to repeat these words of the Kuran: 'God is sufficient for us, and what an excellent Protector.' On that day I repeated this sentence 33,000 times, and I passed the night in the audience chamber. I fasted five days in succession. Every day I read the whole of the Kuran, and I broke my fast only by drinking a little water. The sixth day I took some food, then I fasted four days more in succession, and I was released after the death of the *shaikh*. Thanks be to the Almighty!" His danger had such an effect upon him, that he gave up his offices and went into religious retirement, but the Sultan sent to recall him, and appointed him his ambassador to the King of China. His account of his journey through India to Malabar where he embarked, is full of interesting matter. Dr. Lee made a translation of Ibn Batuta for the Oriental Translation Fund in 1829, but the complete Arabic text with a French translation has since been published by M. M. Defrewand Sanguinetti. It is from this version that the following Extracts have been taken by the Either.

EXTRACTS

The Shaikh Abu 'Abdu-llah Muhammad, son of 'Abdu-llah, son of Muhammad, son of Ibrahim Al Lawati, at Tanji, commonly known as Ibn Batuta, thus declares: —On the 1st of the sacred month of Muharram, 734 H. (12 Sept., 1333), we arrived at the river Sind, the same as is called Pan-jab, a name signifying "Five Rivers." This river is one of the largest known. It overflows in the hot season, and the inhabitants of the country sow their lands after the inundation, as the people of Egypt do after the overflow of the Nile. From this river begin the territories of the great Sultan Muhammad Shah, king of Hind and of Sind. * * *

The *barid* or post in India is of two kinds. The horse-post is called *ulah*, and is carried on by means of horses belonging to the Sultan stationed at every four miles. The foot-post is thus arranged. Each mile is divided into three equal parts, called *dawah*, which signifies one-third of a mile. Among the Indians the mile is called *kos*. At each third of a mile there is a village well populated; outside of which are three tents, in which are men ready to depart. These men gird up their loins, and take in their hands a whip about two cubits long, tipped with brass bells. When the runner leaves the village, he holds the letter in one hand, and in the other the whip with the bells. He runs with all his strength, and when the men in the tents hear the sound of the bells they prepare to receive him. When he arrives, one of them takes the letter and sets off with all speed. He keeps on cracking his whip until he reaches the next *dawah*. Thus, these couriers proceed until the letter reaches its destination.

This kind of post is quicker than the horse-post; and the fruits of Khurasan, which are much sought after in India, are often conveyed by this means. * * * It is by this channel also that great prisoners are transported. They are each placed upon a seat, which the runners take upon their heads and run with. * * *

When the intelligencers inform the Sultan of the arrival of a stranger in his dominions, he takes full notice of the information. The writers do their best to communicate full particulars. They announce the arrival of a stranger, and describe person and his dress. They note the number of his companions, slaves, servants, and beasts. They describe his style of travelling and lodging, and give an account of his expenditure. Not one of these details is passed over. When a traveller arrives at Multan, which is the capital of Sind, he remains there until an order is received from the Sultan for his proceeding to Court and prescribing the kind of treatment he is to receive. * * *

It is the custom of the Sultan of India, Abu-l Mujahid Muhammad Shah, to honour strangers, to favour them, and to distinguish them in a manner quite peculiar, by appointing them to governments or to places of importance. Most of his courtiers, chamberlains, *wazirs*, magistrates, and brothers-in-law are foreigners. * * *

No stranger admitted to Court can avoid offering a present and a kind of introduction, which the Sultan repays by one of much greater value. * * When I arrived in Sind, I observed this practice, and bought some horses, camels, and slaves from the dealers. * * * Two days' march, after crossing the river Sind, we arrived at Janani, a fine large town on the banks of the Sind. It possesses some fine markets, and the Sultan belongs to a race called Samirah [Sumra], who have inhabited that place for a long time, their ancestors having established themselves there since the time of its conquest in the time of Hajjaj, son of Yusuf, as is related by historians in the accounts of the conquest of Sind. * * * The people known by the name of Samirah do not eat with any one, and no one must look at them when they eat. They do not connect themselves in marriage with any other tribe, nor will others ally themselves with them. They had at that time a chief named Unar, whose history I shall relate. * *

We arrived at the imperial residence of Dehli, capital of India, which is a famous and large city uniting beauty and strength. It is surrounded by a wall, the like of which is unknown in the universe. It is the largest city of India, and, in fact, of all the countries subject to Islam in the East.

Description of Dehli

Dehli is a city of great extent, and possesses a numerous population. It consists at present of four neighbouring and contiguous cities.

1. Dehli, properly so called, is the old city built by the idolaters, which was conquered in the year 584 H. (1188 A.D.).

2. Siri, also called Daru-l-Khilafat or Seat of the Khilifat. The Sultan gave it to Ghiyasu-d din, grandson of the Khalif 'Abbaside Al Mustansir, when he came to visit him. Sultan 'Alau-d din and his son Kutbu-d din, of whom we shall have to speak hereafter, dwelt there.

3. Tughlikabad, so called from the name of its founder the Sultan Tughlik, father of the Sultan of India whose Court we are now visiting.* *

4. Jahan-panah, Refuge of the World, specially designed for the residence of the reigning Sultan of India, Muhammad Shah. He built it, and it was his intention to connect all these four cities together by one and the same wall. He raised a portion of it, but abandoned its completion in consequence of the enormous expense its erection would have entailed.

The wall which surrounds Dehli has no equal. It is eleven cubits thick. Chambers are constructed in it which are occupied by the night watch and the persons charged with the care of the gates. In these chambers also there are stores of provisions called *ambar*, magazines of the munitions of war, and others in which are kept mangonels and *ra'adas* ("thunder"—a machine employed in sieges). Grain keeps in these chambers without change or the least deterioration. I saw some rice taken out of one of these magazines; it was black in colour, but good to the taste. I also saw some millet taken out. All these provisions had been stored by Sultan Balban ninety years before. Horse and foot can pass inside this wall from one end of the city to the other. Windows to give light have been opened in it on the inside towards the city. The lower part of the wall is built of stone, the upper part of brick. The bastions are numerous and closely placed. The city of Dehli has twenty-eight gates. First, that of Badaun, which is the principal. * * *

The chief *Kazi* of Hind and Sind, Kamalu-d din Muhammad, son of Burhanu-d din of Ghazni, *Sadr-i-Jahan*, informed me how the city of Dehli was conquered from the infidels in 584 (1188 A.D.). I read the same date inscribed upon the *mihrab* of the great mosque of the city. The same person also informed me that Dehli was taken by the *amir* Kutbu-d din Aibak, who was entitled *Sipah-salar*, meaning General of the armies. He was one of the slaves of the venerated Shahbu-d din Muhammad, son of Sam the Ghorian, king of Ghazni and Khurasan, who had seized upon the kingdom of Ibrahim, son (grandson) of the warlike Mahmud bin Subuktigin, who began the conquest of India.

The aforesaid Shahabu-d din had sent out the *amir* Kutbu-d din with a considerable army. God opened for him the gates of Lahore, where he fixed his residence. His power became considerable. He was calumniated to the Sultan, and the associates of the monarch strove to inspire him with the idea that Kutbu-d din aimed at becoming king of India, and that he was already in open revolt. Intelligence of this reached Kutbu-d din. He set off with all speed, arrived at Ghazni by night, and presented himself to the Sultan, without the knowledge of those who had denounced him. Next day Shahabu-d din took his seat upon the throne, and placed Aibak below, where he was not visible. The courtiers and associates who had maligned Aibak arrived, and when they had all taken their places, the king questioned them about Aibak. They reiterated their statement that Aibak was in revolt, and said, "We know for certain that he aims at royalty." Then the Sultan kicked the foot of the throne, and clapping his hands, cried out "Aibak!" "Here am I," replied he, and came forth before his accusers. They were confounded, and in their terror they hastened to kiss the ground. The Sultan said to them, "I pardon you this time, but beware how you speak against Aibak again." He ordered Aibak to return to India, and he obeyed. He took the city of Dehli, and other cities besides.

Shamsu-d din Altamsh

Shamsu-d din Altamsh was the first who reigned in Dehli with independent power. Before his accession to the throne he had been a slave of the *amir* Kutbu-d din Aibak, the general of his army and his lieutenant. When Kutbu-d din died he assumed the sovereign power, and assembled the population to take from them the oath of allegiance. The lawyers waited upon him, headed by the Kaziu-l Kuzat Wajihu-d din al Kasani. They entered into his pesence and sat down, the *Kaziu-l Kuzat* sitting

down by his side, according to custom. The Sultan knew
what they wanted to speak about. He raised the corner
of the carpet on which he was reclining, and presented to
them the deed of his manumission. The Kazi and the
lawyers read it, and then took the oath of allegiance.
Altamsh became undisputed sovereign, and reigned for
twenty-eight years. He was just, pious, and virtuous.
Among his noteworthy characteristics was the zeal with
which he endeavoured to redress wrongs, and to render
justice to the oppressed. He made an order that any
man who suffered from injustice should wear a coloured
dress. Now all the inhabitants of India wear white
clothes; so whenever he gave audience, or rode abroad,
and saw any one in a coloured dress he inquired into his
grievance, and took means to render him justice against
his oppressor. But he was not satisfied with this plan,
and said: "Some men suffer injustice in the night, and
I wish to give them redress." So he placed at the door of
his palace two marble lions, upon two pedestals which
were there. These lions had an iron chain round their
necks, from which hung a great bell. The victim of injustice came at night and rung the bell, and when the
Sultan heard it, he immediately inquired into the case
and gave satisfaction to the complainant.

Ruknu-d din

At his death Sultan Shamsu-d din left three sons:
Ruknu-d din, who succeeded him; Mu'izzu-d din, and
Nasiru-d din, and one daughter named Raziya, full sister
of Mu'izzu-d din. When Ruknu-d din was recognized as
Sultan, after the death of his father, he began his reign
by unjust treatment of his brother, Mu'izzu-d din, whom
he caused to be put to death. Raziya was full sister of
this unfortunate prince, and she reproached Ruknu-d din
with his death, which made him meditate her assassina-
tion. One Friday he left the palace to go to prayers.
Raziya then ascended to the terrace of the Old Palace,
called Daulat-khana, close by the chief mosque. She was

clothed in the garments of the wronged, and, presenting herself to the people, she addressed them from the terrace, saying, "My brother has killed his brother, and wishes to kill me also." She then reminded them of the reign of her father, and of the many benefits he had bestowed upon them. Thereupon the auditors rushed tumultuously towards Ruknu-d din, who was in the mosque, seized him, and brought him to Raziya. She said, "The slayer must be slain." So they massacred him in retaliation for his murder of his brother. The brother of these two princes, Nasiru-d din, was yet in his infancy, so the people agreed to recognize Raziya as Sovereign.

The Empress Raziya

When Ruknu-d din had been killed, the soldiers agreed to place his sister, Raziya, on the throne. They proclaimed her Sovereign, and she reigned with absolute authority for four years. She rode on horseback as men ride, armed with a bow and quiver, and surrounded with courtiers. She did not veil her face. She was eventually suspected of an intimacy with one of her slaves, an Abyssinian by birth, and the people resolved upon deposing her and giving her a husband. So she was deposed and married to one of her relations, and her brother, Nasiru-d din, obtained the supreme power.

Nasiru-d din, son of Shamsu-d din Altamsh

After the deposition of Raziya, her younger brother, Nasiru-d din, ascended the throne, and for some time exercised royal authority. But Raziya and her husband revolted against him, mounted their horses, and, gathering round them their slaves and such disaffected persons as were willing to join them, they prepared to give battle. Nasiru-d din came out of Dehli with his slave and lieutenant Ghiyasu-d din Balban, who became ruler of the kingdom after him. The opposing forces met, and Raziya was defeated and obliged to fly. Pressed by hunder and overcome with fatigue, she addressed herself to a man engaged in cultivating the ground and begged for food. He gave her a bit of bread, which she devoured, and then she was overpowered by sleep. She was dressed in the garments of a man; but when the peasant looked at her as she slept, he perceived under her upper garment a tunic trimmed with gold and pearls. Seeing she was a woman he killed her, stripped her of her valuables, drove away her horse, and buried her corpse in his field. He then carried some of her garments to the market for sale. The dealers suspected him, and took him before the magistrate, who caused him to be beaten. The wretch then confessed that he had killed Raziya, and told his guards where he had buried her. They exhumed her body, washed it, and, wrapping it in a shroud, buried it again in the same place. A small shrine was erected over her grave, which is visited by pilgrims, and is considered a place of sanctity. It is situated on the banks of the Jumna, about a *parasang* from Dehli.

After the death of his sister, Nasiru-d din remained undisputed master of the State, and reigned in peace for twenty years. He was a religious king. He made copies of the Holy Book and sold them, supporting himself on the money thus obtained. Kazi Kamalu-d din showed me a copy of the Kuran, written by this sovereign, with great taste and elegance. At length his lieutenant, Ghiyasu-d din Balban killed him, and succeeded to his throne.

Sultan Ghiyasu-d din Balban

After Balban had killed his master Nasiru-d din, he reigned with absolute power for twenty years. He had previously been lieutenant of his predecessor for a similar period. He was one of the best of sovereigns—just, clement (*halim*), and good. One of his acts of generosity was this :—He built a house to which he gave the name, "Abode of security." All debtors who entered it had their debts discharged, and whoever in fear fled there for refuge found safety. If a man who had killed another took refuge there, the Sultan bought off the friends of the deceased; and if any delinquent fled there he satisfied those who pursued him. The Sultan was buried in this building, and I have visited his tomb.

* * * The Sultan Shamsu-din Altamsh sent a merchant to buy slaves for him at Samarkand, Bokhara, and Turmuz. This man purchased a hundred slaves, among whom was Balban. When they were presented to the Sultan, they all pleased him except Balban, who was short in stature and of mean appearance. The Sultan exclaimed, "I will not take this one," but the slave cried, "Master of the World, for whom have you bought these servants?" The Sultan laughed and said, "I have bought them for myself." Balban replied, "Then buy me, for the love of God." "Good," exclaimed the Sultan. So he purchased him and placed him with his other slaves.

Balban was treated with contempt, and placed among the water-carriers. Men versed in astrology told the Sultan that one of his slaves would take the kingdom from his son and appropriate it to himself. They continually reiterated this prediction, but the Sultan in his rectitude and justice paid no heed to it. At length they repeated this prediction to the chief queen, mother of the king's sons, and she told the Sultan of it. The words now made an impression upon him, and he sent for the astrologers and said, "Can you recognize, if you see him, the slave who shall deprive my son of the kingdom?" They replied that they had a means by which they could pick him out. The Sultan ordered all his slaves to be brought out, and sat down to review them. They came before him, class after class, and the astrologers looked at them and said, "We have not yet seen him." It was one o'clock in the afternoon, and the water-carriers being hungry, resolved upon collecting a little money and sending some one to the market to purchase food. So they clubbed their *dirhams*, and sent Balban with them, because there was no one among them who was more despised than he. In the market he could not find what his companions wanted, and so he went to another market. This delayed him, and when it came to the turn of the water-carriers to be passed in review, he had not come back. His companions took his water-bottle and pot, and putting them on the back of another youth, presented him as Balban. When the name of Balban was called, this youth passed before the astrologers, and so the review passed over without their finding the person they sought. When the review was over, Balban returned, for it was the will of God that his destiny should be accomplished.

Eventually the noble qualities of the slave were discovered, and he was made chief of the water-carriers. Then he entered the army, and became in course of time an amir. Sultan Nasiru-d din, before he came to the throne, married his daughter, and when he became master of the kingdom he made him his lieutenant. Balban discharged the duties of this office for twenty years, after which he killed his sovereign, and remained master of the empire for twenty years longer, as we have already stated. He had two sons, one of them was "the Martyr Khan," his successor designate, and his viceroy in Sind, where he resided in the city of Multan. He was killed in a war which he carried on against the Tatars and Turks (Mughals). He left two sons Kai-kubad and Kai-khusru. The younger son of Balban was called Nasiru-d din, and ruled as viceroy for his father at Lakhnauti.

Upon the death of "the Martyr Khan," Balban named Kai-khusru, son of the deceased, as heir to the throne, preferring him to his own son Nasiru-d din. The latter had a son named Mu'izzu-d din, who lived at Dehli with his grandfather. This young man, upon the death of his grandfather, and while his father was living, became successor to the throne under the extraordinary circumstances we will now mention.

*Sultan Mu'izzu-d din, son of Nasiru-d din,
son of Sultan Ghiyasu-d din Balban*

Sultan Ghiyasu-d din died in the night while his son Nasiru-d din was at Lakhnauti; after naming as his successor his grandson Kai-khusru, as we have above stated. Now the chief of the *amirs* and deputy of Sultan Ghiyasu-d din was the enemy of this young prince, and he formed a plot against him which succeeded. He drew up a document, in which he forged the hands of the chief *amirs*, attesting that they had taken the oath of allegiance to Mu'izzu-d din, grandson of the deceased Balban. Then he presented himself before Kai-khusru, feigning the greatest interest in him, and said : "The *amirs* have sworn allegiance to your cousin, and I fear their designs against you." Kai-khusru inquired what was best to be done, and the chief of the *amirs* advised him to fly to Sind and save his life. The prince asked how he was to get out of the city, as all the gates were shut ; and the chief *amirs* answered that he had got the keys and would let him out. Kai-khusru thanked him for his offer and kissed his hand. The *amir* advised him to take horse immediately, and so he mounted his horse and was followed by his connexions and slaves. The *amir* opened the gate and let him out, and closed it immediately he had quitted Dehli.

The *amir* then sought an audience of Mu'izzu-d din, and took the oath of submission. The young prince inquired how he could be Sultan, when the title of heir presumptive belonged to his cousin. The chief of the *amirs* then informed him of the ruse he had used against his cousin, and how he had got him to leave the city. Mu'izzu-d din thanked him for his exertions and accompanied him to the palace of the king, where he called together the *amirs* and courtiers who swore allegiance to him in the course of the night. When morning came, the population followed the same course, and the authority of Mu'izzu-d din was firmly established. His Father was still alive, and was in Bengal at Lakhnauti. When he heard of what had taken place, he said, "I am the heir of the kingdom ; how, then, can my son have become master, and have gained absolute power, while I am alive?" He set off for Dehli with his troops. His son also took the field at the head of his army, with the design of repulsing him from Dehli. They met near the town of Karra, on the banks of the Ganges, a place to which Hindus resort in pilgrimate. Nasiru-d din encamped upon the Karra side of the river, and his son, Sultan Mu'izzu-d din, upon the other, so that the river ran between them. They were resolved upon fighting each other; but God wished to spare the blood of Musulmans, and imbued the heart of Nasiru-d din with feelings of pity for his son. So he said to himself, "If my son reigns, it will be an honour to me; it is only right, then, that I should desire that." At the same time God filled the heart of Mu'izzu-d din with sentiments of submission to his father. Each of these two princes entered a boat, and, without any escort of troops, they met in the middle of the river. The Sultan kissed the foot of his father and made his excuses; and the latter replied, "I give thee my kingdom, and confide the government of it thee." Thereupon he took the oath of fidelity, and was about to return to the provinces he possessed, when his son said, "You must certainly come into my kingdom." The father and son proceeded together towards Dehli, and entered the palace. The father placed Mu'izzu-d din upon the throne, and stood before him. The interview which they had upon the river was called "The Conjunction of the Two Auspicious Stars," because of its happy results, in sparing the blood of the people, and in causing the father and son to offer to each other the kingdom, and to abstain from fighting. Many poets have celebrated this incident.

Nasiruld din returned to his territories, and some years after died there, leaving several children, among whom was Ghiyasu-d din Bahadur, whom Sultan Tughlik made prisoner, and whom his son, Muhammad, released after his death. So the kingdom remained in the peaceable possession of Mu'izzu-d din for four years, which were like festival days. I have heard a person who lived at this period describe the happiness, the cheapness of provisions at this time, and the liberality and munificence of Mu'izzu-d din. It was this prince who built the minaret of the northern court of the great mosque at Dehli, which has no equal in the universe. An inhabitant of India informed me that Mu'izzu-d din was much given to the society of women and to drinking; that he was attacked by a malady which defied all the efforts of his physicians to cure, and that one side of him was dried up (paralysis). Then his lieutenant, Jalalu-d din Firoz Shah Khilji, rose up against him.

Sultan Jalalu-d din

When, as we have just described, Sultan Mu'izzu-d din was attacked with hemiplegia, his lieutenant, Jalalu-d din, revolted against him, and, going out of the city, he encamped upon a hill in the neighbourhood, beside a mortuary chapel called Jaishani. Mu'izzu-d din sent out *amirs* to attack him, but all whom he sent with this object swore fidelity to Jalalu-d din, and enrolled themselves in his army. The chief rebel afterwards entered the city and besieged the Sultan in his palace for three days. An eye-witness of the fact informed me that Sultan Mu'izzu-d din suffered from hunger, and could get nothing to eat. One of his neighbours sent him some food to appease his hunger, but the rebellious *amir* forced his way into the palace and Mu'izzu-d din was killed.

Jalalu-d din succeeded. He was an amiable and good man, and his gentleness made him the victim of an assassin, as we shall presently relate. He continued in peaceable possession of the throne for several years, and built the palace which bears his name. It was this building which Sultan Muhammad gave to his brother-in-law, the *amir* Ghada, son of Muhanna, when he married him to his sister, an event which will be spoken of hereafter.

Sultan Jalalu-d din had a son named Ruknu-d din, and a nephew called 'Alau-d din, whom he married to his daughter, and to whom he gave the government of the towns of Karra and Manikpur, with the dependent territories. The wife of 'Alau-d din tormented him, and he was continually complaining of her to his uncle (and father-in-law), Sultan Jalalu-d din, until dissension arose between them on the subject. 'Alau-d din was a sharp and brave man, who had often been victorious, and the ambition of sovereignty took possession of his mind, but he had no wealth but what he won by the point of his sword by despoiling the infidels. He set out to carry the holy war into the country of Deogir (or Daulatabad), which is also called the country of Kataka, of which mention will be made hereafter. Deogir is the capital of Malwa and of Marhata (the country of the Mahrattas), and its ruler was the most powerful of all the infidel kings. In the course of this expedition, the horse of 'Alau-d din stumbled against a stone and threw his rider. 'Alau-d din heard a sort of jingling noise made by the stone. He ordered the place to be dug up, and a considerable treasure was found under the stone, which he divided among his companions. When he arrived at Deogir, the ruler submitted and surrendered the city without fighting, making valuable presents to his conqueror. 'Alau-d din returned to Karra, but did not send any portion of the spoil to his uncle. Certain persons stirred up the feelings of his uncle against him, and the Sultan summoned him. He refused to go to Court, and the Sultan then said, "I will go and bring him, for he is to me as a son." Accordingly he set out with his army, and marched until he reached the bank of the river opposite to Karra, at the same place where Sultan Mu'izzu-d din had encamped when he went to meet his father, Nasiru-d din. He embarked on the river to go and meet his nephew. The latter also took boat with the intention of making an end of the Sultan, and he said to his companions, "When I embrace him, kill him." When the two princes met in the middle of the river, the nephew embraced his uncle, and his companions despatched the Sultan as he had instructed them. The murderer seized upon the kingdom, and took command of the troops of his victim.

Sultan 'Alau-d din Muhammad Shah Khilji

When he had killed his uncle he became master of the kingdom, and the greater part of the troops of Jalalu-d din passed over to his side. The rest returned to Dehli and gathered round Ruknu-d din. The latter marched out to attack the murderer, but all his soldiers deserted to 'Alau-d din; and he fled to Sind. 'Alau-d din took possession of the palace and reigned peaceably for twenty years. He was one of the best of Sultans, and the people of India eulogize him highly. He personally examined the affairs of his people, and inquired into the price of provisions. Every day the *muhtasib*, or inspector of the markets, whom the Indians called *rais* or chief, had to attend before him. It is said that one day he questioned the inspector about the dearness of meat, and he was told that it arose from the high tax upon bullocks. He ordered the tax to be abolished and the dealers to be brought before him. He gave them money, and said, "With this buy bullocks and sheep, and sell them; the price that they fetch must be paid to the treasury, and you shall receive an allowance for selling them." This (order) was carried into execution. And the Sultan acted in a similar way in respect of the fabrics brought from Daulatabad. When corn reached a high price he opened the granaries of the State, and sold their stores, until the price came down. It is said that on one occasion the price of corn rose, and he ordered the dealers to sell it at a price which he fixed. They refused to sell it at the price named. He then ordered that nobody should purchase grain except at the government stores, and he sold it to the people for six months. The monopolists were afraid that their stocks would be devoured by weevils, and they begged permission to sell. The Sultan gave them leave, but upon condition that they sold at a price lower than they had before refused.

'Alau-d din never rode on horseback, either to go to public prayer on Fridays, or on festivals, or on any occasion whatever. The reason of this was that he had a nephew, named Sulaiman Shah, whom he loved and favoured. One day he mounted his horse to go a-hunting with this nephew, and this one conceived the idea of dealing with his uncle as he, 'Alau-d din, had dealt with his uncle Jalalu-d din, that is, of assassinating him. So when the Sultan alighted to take breakfast, he discharged an arrow at him and brought him down, but a slave covered him with a shield. The nephew came up to finish him, but the slaves told him that he was dead. He, believing them, rode off and entered the women's apartments in the palace. The Sultan recovered from his fainting fit, mounted his horse, and gathered together his troops. His nephew fled, but he was captured and brought before the Sultan. He slew him, and after that ceased to ride on horseback.

'Alau-d din had several sons, whose names were—1. Khizr Khan, 2. Shadi Khan, 3. Abu Bakr Khan, 4. Mubarak Khan, also called Kutbu-d din, who became king, 5. Shahabu-d din. Kutbu-d din was treated unkindly by his father, and received very little notice. The Sultan bestowed honours on all his brothers—that is, he granted them banners and drums; but on him he conferred nothing. But one day the Sultan said to him, "I really must give you what I have given your brothers." Kutbu-d din replied, "It is God who will give it me." This answer alarmed his father, who became afraid of him. The Sultan was then attacked by the malady of which he died. The wife by whom he had his son Khizr Khan, and who was called Mah-hakk, had a brother named Sanjar, with whom she conspired to raise Khizr Khan to the throne. Malik Naib, the chief of the Sultan's *amirs*, who was called Al Alfi,[2] because his master had bought him for 1,000 (*alf*) *tankas*, that is, 2,500 African *dinars*. This Malik Naib got knowledge of the plot and informed the Sultan. Thereupon he gave his attendants this order: "When Sanjar enters the room where I am, I will give him a robe. As he is putting it on, seize him by the sleeves,

* *Haur dinari.*

throw him down, and despatch him." This order was exactly executed.

Khizr Khan was then absent at a place called Sandabat (Sonpat), one day's journey from Dehli, whether he had gone on a pilgrimage to the tombs of certain martyrs buried there. He had made a vow to walk thither on foot, and pray for the health of his father. But when Khizr Khan heard that his father had killed his maternal uncle, he was greatly concerned, and tore the collar of his garment, as the Indians are in the habit of doing when any one dies who is dear to them. His father, on hearing this, was much annoyed, and when Khizr Khan appeared before him, he reprimanded and censured him. Then he ordered irons to be put upon his hands and feet, and gave him into the charge of Malik Naib above mentioned, with orders to convey him to the fortress of Gwalior. This is an isolated fort, in the midst of idolatrous Hindus, at ten days' journey from Dehli, and it is impregnable. I resided there some time. When Malik Naib took the prince to this strong fort, he gave him into the charge of the *kotwal*, or the commandant, and of the *mufrids* or *zamanis* (regularly enrolled soldiers), and told them not to say that their prisoner was the son of the Sultan, but to treat him honourably. He was the Sultan's most bitter enemy, so they were to guard him as an enemy.

Finally, the Sultan's malady growing worse, he told Malik Naib to send some one to fetch Khizr Khan, that he might proclaim him his successor. Malik Naib acquiesced, but he delayed from day to day to execute the order, and whenever his master inquired about the matter, he replied that his son would soon arrive. He continued to act thus until the Sultan died.

Sultan Shahabu-d din, son of 'Alau-d din

When the Sultan 'Alau-d din was dead, Malik Naib raised his younger son, Shahabu-d din, to the throne. The people took the oath of obedience to him, but Malik

Naib kept him under his own direction, and after depriving Abu Bakr Khan and Shadi Khan of sight, he sent them to Gwalior. He also ordered their brother Khizr Khan, who was imprisoned in the same place, to be blinded. They were imprisoned, as well as Kutbu-d din, but the minister spared the sight of the latter. Sultan 'Alau-d din had two slaves, who were his personal attendants; one was called Bashir and the other Mubashir. The chief princess, widow of 'Alau-d din, and daughter of Sultan Mu'izzu-d din, sent for them, recounted the benefits which they had received from their late master, and said, "This eunuch, Malik Naib, has treated my children in the way you know of, and now he wants to kill Kutbu-d din." They replied, "You shall see what we will do." It was usual for them to pass the night near Malik Naib, and to enter armed into his presence. They went to wait upon him the following night in his *Khurram-gah*, as the Indians call a kind of room constructed of planks and hung with cloth. Here the *wazir* slept;—on the terrace of the palace during the rainy season. It so happened that he took the sword worn by one of these conspirators, brandished it, and returned it. The slave then struck him with it, and his companion gave him another blow. Then they cut off his head, and, carrying it to the prison of Kutbu-d din, and throwing it down at his feet, delivered him from captivity. The prince went and joined his brother, Shahabu-d din, and stayed with him several days, as if he had been his lieutenant, but at length he resolved to depose him, and carried out his design.

Sultan Kutbu-d din, son of Sulltan 'Alau-d din

This prince deposed his brother Shahabu-d din, cut off one of his fingers, and sent him to Gwalior, where he was imprisoned with his brothers. The kingdom came peaceably into the hands of Kutbu-d din, who left Dehli, his capital, to proceed to Daulatabad, forty days' journey distant. The road between these two places is bordered with trees, such as the willow and others, so that the traveller might think himself in a garden. In the space of every mile there are three *dawas*, or posting-houses, of which the arrangements have been already described. At each of these stations the traveller finds all that he needs, as if his forty days' journey lay through a market. Thus the road goes on for six months' journey, till it reaches the country of Tilang and Ma'bar. At every station there is a palace for the Sultan and a corner for the traveller, and poor people have no need to carry with them provisions for their journey.

After Sultan Kutbu-d din had set off on this expedition, certain *amirs* determined among themselves to revolt against him, and to place a son of his imprisoned brother Khizr Khan upon the throne. This child was about ten years old, and was near the Sultan. When the latter heard of this plot of the *amirs*, he took his nephew, seized him by the feet, and dashed his head against the stones till his brains were scattered. He then sent an *amir*, named Malik Shah, to Gwalior, where the father and uncles of the child were confined, with orders to kill them all. Kazi Zainu-d din Mubarak, *kazi* of this stronghold, gave me the following account:—"Malik Shah reached us one morning, whilst, I was with Khizr Khan in his prison. When the captive heard of his arrival, he was frightened, and changed colour. The *amir* came in, and he said to him, 'Why have you come?' and he answered, 'Upon a matter which concerns the Lord of the World.' The prince asked if his life was safe, and he answered 'Yes.' Thereupon the *amir* went out and called for the *kotwal*, or commandant, and his *mufrids*, or soldiers, to the number of 300; he sent for me, as well as the notaries, and produced the order of the Sultan. The men of the garrison read it, then went to Shahabu-d din, the deposed Sultan, and cut off his head. He was very collected, and showed no sign of fear. Then they beheaded Abu Bakr and Shadi Khan. When they went to decapitate Khizr Khan, he was overcome with fear and stupor. His mother was with him, but the executioners shut the door against her and killed him. Then they dragged the four bodies to a ditch, without either wrapping them in shrouds or washing them. They were exhumed after some years and were interred in the tombs of their ancestors." The mother of Khizr Khan survived some time. I saw her at Mecca in the year 728 H. (A.D. 1327).

The fort of Gwalior here spoken of is situated on the top of a high mountain, and appears, so to speak, to be cut out of the rock itself. There is no other mountain in face of it. There are subterranean cisterns in it, and it contains also about twenty bricked wells. *Manjaniks* and *'arradas* are mounted on the walls. The passage to the fortress is up a spacious road, which elephants and horses can ascend. Near the gate of the fort there is the figure of an elephant, sculptured in stone, carrying its driver. When seen from a distance, it seems to be a real elephant. At the base of the fortress there is a fine town, built entirely of white hewn stone, mosques and houses alike. No wood is seen except in the doors. It is the same with the palace of the king, the domes and halls. Most of the business men of this town are idolaters, and there are about 600 horsemen of the royal army there, who never cease to fight with the infidels by whom the place is surrounded.

When Kutbu-d din had killed his brothers, and he had become sole master, without any one left to fight with him or revolt against him, God raised up against him his favourite servant, the most powerful of his *amirs* and the highest in dignity, Nasiru-d din Khusru Khan. This 'man' attacked him unawares, killed him, and remained absolute master of the kingdom. But this did not last long. God raised also against him one who dethroned and then killed him. This was the Sultan Tughlik, as will hereafter be fully recorded, God willing!

Khusru Khan Nasiru-d din

Khusru Khan was one of the principal *amirs* of

Kutbu-d din. He was brave and handsome. He had conquered the country of Chanderi, and also that of Ma'bar, which are among the most fertile regions of India, and are at a distance of six months' journey from Dehli. Kutbu-d din liked this man very much, and showed great fondness for him;—this was the cause of the Sultan's meeting death at his hands. * * * One day Khusru Khan told the Sultan that several Hindus desired to become Musulmans. It is one of the customs in this country that, when a person wishes to become a convert to Islam, he is brought before the king, who gives him a fine robe and a necklace and bracelets of gold, proportionate in value to his rank. The Sultan told Khusru to bring the Hindus before him, but the *amir* replied that they were ashamed to come by day on account of their relations and co-religionists. So the Sultan told him to bring them at night.

Khusru Khan gathered a troop of Indians, chosen from among the bravest and greatest; his brother, the *Khan-i Khanan*, was among them. It was the hot season, and the Sultan slept on the roof of the palace, having only a few eunuchs around him. When the Indians bearing their weapons had passed four gates of the palace and arrived at the fifth, Kazi Khan, the keeper of the keys, was startled by their proceedings, and suspected that they had some evil design in view. So he prevented their entrance, and said he would not let them pass without a distinct order from the mouth of the king himself. Finding themselves thus stopped, they fell upon him and killed him. The noise arising from this contention grew loud and reached the Sultan, who asked what it was, and Khusru Khan told him that it was made by the Indians, who were coming to make their profession. Kazi Khan had opposed their entrance, and hence a tumult had arisen. The Sultan was alarmed and rose to go into the inner part of the palace, but the door was closed and the eunuchs stood near it. The Sultan knocked at the door. Khusra Khan then seized him in his arms from behind, but the king was the stronger and threw him down. The Indians entered, and Khusru Khan called out to them, "Here he is upon me, kill him!" So they murdered him and cut off his head, which they threw from the roof of the palace into the court-yard.

Khusru Khan sent immediately for the *amirs* and *maliks* who were not yet aware of what had happened. Each party that entered found him seated on the throne. They took the oath (of allegiance) to him, and when morning came he proclaimed his accession, despatched his orders into all the provinces, and sent a robe of honour to each *amir*. They all submitted to him with the exception of Tughlik Shah, father of Sultan Muhammad Shah, who was then governor of Dibalpur, in Sind. When he received the robe of honour which Khusru had allotted to him, he threw it on the ground and sat upon it. Khusru Khan sent his brother, the *Khan-i Khanan*, against him, but Tughlik defeated him and afterwards killed him, as will be narrated in the account of the reign of Tughlik.

Khusru Khan, upon becoming king, showed great favour to the Hindus, and issued objectionable orders, such as an order prohibiting the slaughter of bullocks, in deference to the practice of the idolatrous Indians, who do not allow these animals to be killed. * * * Such conduct was one of the causes which made Khusru Khan hateful to the Musulmans, and made them incline in favour of Tughlik. Khusru's reign did not last long, and the days of his power were not numerous, as we shall relate.

Sultan Ghiyasu-d din Tughlik Shah

The *shaikh* and pious *imam* Ruknu-d din * * * gave me the following account in his hermitage at Multan. Sultan Tughlik belonged to the race of Turks called *Karauna*,[1] who inhabit the mountains between Sind and

[1] See Jour. Asiatique, Tome II., 1844, pp. 515, 517. D'Ohsson Hist. des Mongols, IV., p. 46.

the country of the Turks. He was in a very humble condition, and went to Sind as servant of a certain merchant, as his *golwani*, or groom. This took place in the reign of 'Alau-d din, whose brother, Ulu Khan,[a] was governor of Sind. Tughlik entered his service and was attached to his person, being enrolled among his *piadas* or footmen. Afterwards he distinguished himself by his bravery, and was entered among the horsemen; then he became a subordinate *amir*, and Ulu Khan made him his master of the horse. Finally, he became one of the great *amirs*, and received the title of *al malik al ghazi*, "warlike prince." I have seen the following inscription, which is placed over the sacrarium of the mosque which he built at Multan: "I have fought with the Tatars twenty-nine times, and have defeated them. It is for this that I have been called 'the warlike prince.'"

When Kutbu-d din became king, he made Tughlik governor of the town and district of Dibalpur; and he made his son (the present Sultan of India) superintendent of the imperial stables. He was called *Jauna*, the Sun; when he became king he called himself Muhammad Shah. Kutbu-d din being dead, and Khusru Khan having succeeded, he confirmed Jauna in his office as master of the horse. When Tughlik wanted to rebel, he had 300 comrades in whom he put confidence in the day of battle. He wrote to Kishlu Khan, who was then at Multan, three days' journey from Dibalpur, calling upon him for assistance, reminding him of the favours of Kutbu-d din, and urging him to exact vengeance for the murder of that king. The son of Kishlu Khan resided at Dehli, and, consequently, he replied to Tughlik that if his son were with him he would certainly help his design. Tughlik wrote to his son, Muhammad Shah, to inform him of his resolves, and desiring him to fly from Dehli to meet him, bringing with him the son of Kishlu Khan. The young nobleman contrived a stratagem against Khusru Khan, which was successful. He told him that the horses had

[a] Ulugh Khan.

grown fat and heavy, and that they required exercise. Khusru Khan accordingly gave permission for taking them out. So the master of the horse mounted on horseback every day, and, followed by his subordinates, he rode about from one to three hours; he even extended his absence to four hours, so that one day he was out till noon had passed, which is the time when the Indians dine. The Sultan sent out to look after him, but nothing could be heard of him, and he joined his father, together with the son of Kishlu Khan.

Tughlik then openly rebelled and collected his forces. Kishlu Khan also joined him with his soldiers. The Sultan sent out his brother, the *Khan-i Khanan*, to give them battle, but they totally defeated him, and his army passed over to their side. The *Khan-i Khanan* returned to his brother; his officers were slain and his treasure captured. Tughlik then proceeded towards Dehli. Khusru Khan went out to meet him with his army, and encamped near the city at a place called Asya-bad. that is to say, the windmill. He ordered the treasures to be opened, and he gave away the money by bags, not by weight or definite sums. The battle began between him and Tughlik, and the Indians fought with the greatest fury. Tughlik's troops were defeated, his camp was pillaged, and he remained surrounded by his 300 old companions. He cried, "Whither can we fly? We shall be taken everywhere and killed." The soldiers of Khusru were busy plundering, and were scattered, so that there remained only a few near him. Tughlik and his companions went against him. In this country the presence of the sovereign is always indicated by the umbrella carried over his head.

When Tughlik and his companions advanced against Khusru, the fight began again between them and the Hindus; the Sultan's troops were routed, and none remained near him. He took to flight, dismounted from his horse, threw away his garments and arms, and keeping only his shirt, he let his hair fall upon his shoulders as the *fakirs* of India do. Then he went into a garden near at hand. The people gathered round Tughlik, who proceeded towards the city. The governor brought him the keys. He entered the palace and lodged in one of its wings; then he said to Kishlu Khan, "Be thou Sultan!" The Khan replied, "Rather you." They disputed together, but at length Kishlu Khan said to Tughlik, "If you refuse to be Sultan, your son will obtain the sovereign power." Tughlik was averse to this, so he accepted the government, and sat upon the royal throne. The nobles and common people took their oaths to him.

After three days Khusru Khan, still concealed in the same garden, was hard pressed by hunger. He came out of his hiding-place and walked about. Then he met the keeper of the garden, and asked him for some food. The man had none to give him, so Khusru gave him his ring and told him to go and pawn it, and buy food. When this person went into the market with the ring, the people had their suspicions, and they took him to the police magistrate. The latter conducted him to Tughlik, to whom he made known who had given him the ring. Tughlik sent his son Muhammad to bring in Khusru, and Muhammad seized him, placed him on a *tatu*, or baggage-horse, and brought him to his father. When Khusru went into the presence of Tughlik, he said: "I am hungry, give me something to eat." The new sovereign ordered him to be served with *sharbat*, food, beer, and lastly betel. When he had eaten he rose and said, "O Tughlik, deal with me after the manner of kings, and do not dishonour me." Tughlik complied with his request; he ordered him to be beheaded, and he was executed on the very spot where he had killed Kutbu-d din. His head and his body were thrown from the roof of the palace, as he had done with the head of his predecessor. Afterwards, Tughlik ordered his corpse to be washed, wrapped in a shroud, and buried in a tomb which he himself had built. Tughlik was a just and excellent prince, and he enjoyed the sovereign power in peace for four years.

When Tughlik was firmly established in his capital, he sent his son, Muhammad, to make the conquest of Tilang, three months' march from Dehli. He sent with him a considerable army, attached to which were the principal *amirs*, such as Malik Timur, Malik Tigin, Malik Kafur the seal-bearer, Malik Bairam, and others. When Muhammad arrived in Tilang, he was desirous of revolting. He had for a companion a man called 'Ubaid, who was a poet and lawyer. He ordered him to spread a report of the Sultan Tughlik being dead, for he supposed that all men, on hearing this intelligence, would in hot haste tender him their oath of fidelity. This news spread among the soldiers, but the *amirs* did not believe it. Every one of them beat his drums and revolted. No one remained near Muhammad, and the chiefs wished to kill him. Malik Timur prevented them, and protected him. He fled to his father with ten horsemen, whom he called his "faithful friends." His father gave him money and troops, and commanded him to return to Tilang, and he obeyed. But the Sultan was acquainted with his design; he killed the lawyer 'Ubaid, and he ordered Malik Kafur, the seal-bearer, to be put to death. A tent peg was driven into the ground, and the upper end of it was sharpened. This was driven into the throat of Kafur, who was placed thereon, face downwards, and it came out by one of his ribs. Thus he was left. The other *amirs* fled to Sultan Shamsu-d din, son of Sultan Nasiru-d din, son of Sultan Ghiyasu-d din Balban, and established themselves at his Court (at Lakhnauti).

The fugitive *amirs* dwelt with Sultan Shamsu-d din. Soon afterwards he died, leaving his throne to his son, Shahabu-d din. This prince succeeded his father, but his younger brother, Ghiyasu din Bahadur Burah (this last word signifies in the Indian language *black*), overpowered him, seized upon the kingdom, and killed his brother Katlu Khan, and most of his other brothers. Two of them, Sultan Shahabu-d din and Nasiru-d din, fled to Tughlik, who marched forth with them to fight with the fratricide. He left his son Muhammad in his kingdom as viceroy, and advanced in haste to the country of Lakhnauti. He subdued it, made the Sultan Ghiyasu-d din prisoner, and set off on the march to his capital, carrying his prisoner with him.

There was then at Dehli a saint, Nizamu-d din Badauni. Muhammad, the Sultan's son, often visited him, to pay him respect in the eyes of his followers and to implore his prayers. The *shaikh* was subject to ecstatic fits, in which he lost all control of himself. The Sultan's son directed his servants to let him know when the *shaikh* was in one of these fits. When he was seized with a fit the prince was informed, and he went to him. As soon as the *shaikh* saw him he exclaimed, "We give him the throne." Afterwards he died while the Sultan was absent, and the Sultan's son, Muhammad, bore his bier upon his shoulder. The father heard of this; he suspected his son and threatened him. Other actions had already aroused suspicions in Tughlik against his son. He was annoyed to see him buy a great number of slaves, and make magnificent presents to secure friends. Now his anger against him increased. The Sultan was informed that the astrologers had predicted that he would never enter again the city of Dehli on returning from his expedition. He replied by threats against them.

When he came near to his capital, on his return from the expedition, he ordered his son to build for him a palace, or, as these people call it, a *kushk*, near a river, which runs by a place called Afghanpur. Muhammad built it in the course of three days, making it chiefly of wood. It was elevated above the ground, and rested on pillars of wood. Muhammad planned it scientifically, and Malik Zada was charged to see the plans carried out. This man was afterwards known by the title of Khwaja-i Jahan. His real name was Ahmad, son of Ayas. He was then inspector of buildings, but he afterwards became chief *wazir* of Sultan Muhammad. The object which these two persons kept in view in building the *kushk* was this,—that it should fall down with a crash when the elephants touched it in a certain part. The Sultan stopped at this building and feasted the people, who afterwards dispersed. His son asked permission to parade the elephants before him, fully accoutred. The Sultan consented.

Shaikh Ruknu-d din told me that he was then near the Sultan, and that the Sultan's favourite son, Mahmud, was with them. Thereupon Muhammad came and said to the *shaikh*, "Master, it is now the time for afternoon prayer, go down and pray." I went down, said the *shaikh*, and they brought the elephants up on one side, as the prince and his confidant had arranged. When the animals passed along that side, the building fell down upon the Sultan and his son Mahmud. I heard the noise, continued the *shaikh*, and I returned without having said my prayer. I saw that the building had fallen. The Sultan's son, Muhammad, ordered pickaxes and shovels to be brought to dig and seek for his father, but he made signs for them not to hurry, and the tools were not brought till after sunset. Then they began to dig, and they found the Sultan, who had bent over his son to save him from death. Some assert that Tughlik was taken out dead; others, on the contrary, maintain that he was alive, and that an end was made of him. He was carried away at night to the tomb which he had himself built near the city called after him Tughlikabad, and there he was interred. * * *

It was to the skilful management of the *wazir*, Khwaja-i Jahan, in constructing the edifice which fell upon Tughlik, that he owed the position he held with Sultan Muhammad, and the partiality which the latter had for him. No one, whether *wazir* or otherwise, enjoyed anything like the consideration in which he was held by the Sultan, and never attained the high position which he possessed near him.

Sultan Abu-l Mujahid Muhammad Shah

When the Sultan Tughlik was dead, his son Muhammad took possession of the kingdom, without encountering either adversary or rebel. As we have said above, his name was Jauna; but when he became king he called himself Muhammad, and received the surname of Abu-l Mujahid. All that I have recounted about the history of the Sultans of India, I heard and learned, or, at least, the greater part, from the mouth of Shaikh Kamalu-d din, son of Burhanu-d din, of Ghazni, chief kazi. As to the adventures of this king, the greater part came under my own observation while living in his territories.

Muhammad is a man who, above all others, is fond of making presents and shedding blood. There may always be seen at his gate some poor person becoming rich, or some living one condemned to death. His generous and brave actions, and his cruel and violent deeds, have obtained notoriety among the people. In spite of this, he is the most humble of men, and the one who exhibits the greatest equity. The ceremonies of religion are dear to his heart, and he is very severe in respect of prayer and the punishment which follows its neglect. He is one of those kings whose good fortune is great, and whose happy success exceeds the ordinary limit; but his distinguishing characteristic is generosity. I shall mention among the instances of his liberality, some marvels of which the like has never been reported of any of the princes who have preceded him. I call God, his angels and prophets, to witness that all I say about his boundless munificence is the plain truth. * * *

The palace of the Sultan at Dehli is called Darsara, and it has a great number of gates. At the first there is a troop of men posted on guard. * * * Outside the first gate there are stages on which the executioners sit who have to kill people. It is the custom with this people that whenever the Sultan orders the execution of a person, he is despatched at the door of the hall of audience, and his body remains there three days. * * * The third door abuts upon the hall of audience, an immense chamber called *Hazar-sutun*, or "the thousand columns." These pillars are of varnished wood, and support a wooden roof painted in the most admirable style. Here people seat themselves, and in this hall the Sultan holds his great public audiences. [*Etiquette of the Court.* —*Many instances of the Sultan's liberality and generosity.*]

When drought prevailed throughout India and Sind, and the scarcity was so great that the *man* of wheat was worth six *dinars*, the Sultan gave orders that provisions for six months should be supplied to all the inhabitants of Dehli from the royal granaries. * * * The officers of justice made registers of the people of the different streets, and these being sent up, each person received sufficient provisions to last him for six months.

The Sultan, notwithstanding all I have said about his humility, his justice, his kindness to the poor, and his boundless generosity, was much given to bloodshed. It rarely happened that the corpse of some one who had been killed was not to be seen at the gate of his palace. I have often seen men killed and their bodies left there. One day I went to his palace and my horse shied. I looked before me, and I saw a white heap on the ground, and when I asked what it was, one of my companions said it was the trunk of a man cut into three pieces. This sovereign punished little faults like great ones, and spared neither the learned, the religious, nor the noble. Every day hundreds of individuals were brought chained into his hall of audience; their hands tied to their necks and their feet bound together. Some were killed, and others were tortured, or well beaten. It was his practice to have all persons in prison brought before him every day except Friday. This day was to them a day of respite, and they passed it in cleaning themselves and taking rest. God preserve us from evil!

8

The Sultan's murder of his brother

The Sultan had a brother named Mas'ud Khan, whose mother was a daughter of Sultan 'Alau-d din. This Mas'ud was one of the handsomest fellows I have ever seen. The king suspected him of intending to rebel, so he questioned him, and, under fear of the torture, Mas'ud confessed the charge. Indeed, every one who denies charges of this nature, which the Sultan brings against him, is put to the torture, and most people prefer death to being tortured. The Sultan had his brother's head cut off in the palace, and the corpse, according to custom, was left neglected for three days in the same place. The mother of Mas'ud had been stoned two years before in the same place on a charge of debauchery or adultery.

* * *

On one occasion the Sultan sent a part of his army, under Malik Yusuf Bughra, to fight against the Hindus in the mountains near Dehli. Yusuf started with nearly all his men, but some of the soldiers stayed behind. He wrote to the Sovereign informing him of the fact, and he directed search to be made throughout the city, and every man who had remained behind to be apprehended. Three hundred of them were taken. The Sultan ordered all of them to be killed, and he was obeyed.

Destruction of Dehli

One of the most serious charges against this Sultan is that he forced all the inhabitants of Dehli to leave their homes. His motive for this act was that the people of Dehli wrote letters full of insults and invectives against the Sultan. They sealed them up, and writing upon them these words, "By the head of the king of the world, no one but himself must read this writing," they threw them at night into the hall of audience. When the Sultan opened them he found that they contained insults and invectives against himself. He decided to ruin Dehli, so he purchased all the houses and inns from the inhabitants, paid them the price, and then ordered them to remove to Daulatabad. At first they were unwilling to obey, but the crier of the monarch proclaimed that no one must be found in Dehli after three days.

The greater part of the inhabitants departed, but some hid themselves in the houses. The Sultan ordered a rigorous search to be made for any that remained. His slaves found two men in the streets: one was paralyzed, the other blind. They were brought before the sovereign, who ordered the paralytic to be shot away from a *manjanik*, and the blind man to be dragged from Dehli to Daulatabad. All the inhabitants of Dehli left; they abandoned their baggage and their merchandize, and the city remained a perfect desert.

A person in whom I felt confidence assured me that the Sultan mounted one evening upon the roof of his palace, and, casting his eyes over the city of Dehli, in which there was neither fire, smoke, nor light, he said, "Now my heart is satisfied, and my feelings are appeased." Some time after he wrote to the inhabitants of different provinces, commanding them to go to Dehli and repeople it. They ruined their own countries, but they did not populate Dehli, so vast and immense is that city. In fact, it is one of the greatest cities in the universe. When we entered this capital we found it in the state which has been described. It was empty, abandoned, and had but a small population.

Rebellion of Bahau-d din

Sultan Tughlik had a nephew, son of his sister, named Bahau-d din Gushtasp, whom he made governor of a province. This man was a brave warrior, a hero; and when his uncle was dead he refused to give his oath to the late Sultan's son and successor. The Sultan sent a force against him; * * * there was a fierce battle, * * * and the Sultan's troops gained the victory. Bahau-d din fled to one of the Hindu princes, called the Rai of Kambila. * * * This prince had territories situated among inaccessible mountains, and was one of the chief princes of the infidels.

When Bahau-d din made his escape to this prince, he was pursued by the soldiers of the Sultan of India, who surrounded the *rai's* territories. The infidel saw his danger, for his stores of grain were exhausted, and his great fear was that the enemy would carry off his person by force; so he said to Bahau-d din, "Thou seest how we are situated. I am resolved to die with my family, and with all who will imitate me. Go to such and such a prince (naming a Hindu prince), and stay with him; he will defend thee." He sent some one to conduct him thither. Then he commanded a great fire to be prepared and lighted. Then he burned his furniture, and said to his wives and daughters, "I am going to die, and such of you as prefer it, do the same." Then it was seen that each one of these women washed herself, rubbed her body with sandal-wood, kissed the ground before the *rai* of Kambila, and threw herself upon the pile. All perished. The wives of his nobles, ministers, and chief men imitated them, and other women also did the same.

The *rai*, in his turn, washed, rubbed himself with sandal, and took his arms, but did not put on his breast-plate. Those of his men who resolved to die with him followed his example. They sallied forth to meet the troops of the Sultan, and fought till every one of them fell dead. The town was taken, its inhabitants were made prisoners, and eleven sons of the *rai* were made prisoners and carried to the Sultan, who made them all Musulmans. The Sultan made them *amirs*, and treated them with great honour, as much for their illustrious birth as in admiration of the conduct of their father. Of these brothers, I saw near the Sultan, Nasr. Bakhtiyar, and the keeper of the seals, who carried the ring with which the Sultan's drinking-water was sealed. His name was Abu Muslim, and we were companions and friends.

After the death of the *rai* of Kambila, the troops of the Sultan proceeded towards the country of the infidel with whom Bahau-d din had taken refuge, and surrounded it. This prince said, "I cannot do as the *rai* of Kambila did." He seized Bahau-d din, and gave him up to the army of the Sultan. They bound his legs and tied his arms to his neck, and so conducted him to the Sultan. He ordered the prisoner to be taken to the women, his relations, and these insulted him and spat upon him. Then he ordered him to be skinned alive, and as his skin was torn off his flesh was cooked with rice. Some was sent to his children and his wife, and the remainder was put into a great dish and given to the elephants to eat, but they would not touch it. The Sultan ordered his skin to be stuffed with straw, and to be placed along with the remains of Bahadur Bura,[a] and to be exhibited throughout the country. When these arrived in Sind, of which country Kishlu Khan was then governor, he ordered them to be buried. When the Sultan heard this he was offended, and determined to make away with Kishlu Khan, who was the friend of Sultan Tughlik, and had helped him in obtaining the supreme power.

Rebellion of Kishlu Khan

As soon as the Sultan was informed of what Kishlu Khan had done in the matter of burying the two skins, he sent for him. Kishlu Khan instantly understood that the Sultan intended to punish him, so he did not attend to the invitation. He revolted, spread his money about, raised troops, and sent emissaries among the Turks, Afghans, and Khurasanians, who flocked to him in great numbers. His army was equal to that of the Sultan, or even superior to it in numbers. The Sovereign marched in person to fight him, and they met at two day's journey from Multan, in the desert plain of Abubar. In this battle the Sultan showed great prudence. He placed

---

[a] Ghiyasu-d din Bahadur Bura, King of Bengal, whom he restored to his kingdom, and afterwards defeated and killed. The skin of this victim was torn off and stuffed.

Shaikh 'Imadu-d din, who resembled him (in person), under the royal canopy, whilst he himself moved off during the heat of the battle with 4,000 men. The enemy endeavoured to take the canopy, thinking it was the Sovereign who was under it. 'Imadu-i din was killed, and they thought that the Sultan had perished. The soldiers of Kishlu Khan were intent only on plunder, and separated from their chief, who was left with only a few men. Then the Sultan fell upon him and cut off his head. When Kishlu Khan's troops knew this, they took to flight.

The Sultan then entered Multan, where he seized the *kazi*, Karimu-d din, and ordered him to be flayed alive. He brought with him the head of Kishlu Khan, which he caused to be suspended over his own door. I saw it there when I arrived in Multan.

Disaster suffered by the army in the mountain of Karachil (in the Himalayas)

This is a vast mountain, three months' journey in length, and ten days' journey from Dehli. Its king was one of the most powerful of the Hindu princes, and the Sultan of India sent an army to fight with him, commanded by Malik Nakbia, chief of the inkstand bearers. The army consisted of 100,000 horse and a large number of infantry. They took the town of Jidiya, situated at the foot of the mountain, and the places adjacent, making prisoners, plundering, and burning. The infidels fled to the heights of the mountain, abandoning their country, their flocks, and the treasures of their king. The mountain has only one road. Below lies a valley; above, the mountain itself; and horsemen can only pass one by one. The troops of the Sultan ascended by this road, and took possession of the town of Warangal, in the upper part of the mountain. They seized upon everything it contained, and wrote to their Sovereign informing him of their victory. He sent them a *kazi* and a preacher, and ordered them to remain in the country.

When the great rains came on, the army was attacked by disease, which considerably weakened it. The horses died, and the bows grew slack, so the *amirs* sought permission from the Sultan to leave the mountain during the rainy season, to descend to its base, and to again take up their position when the rains had ceased. The Sultan consented. So the commander Nakbia took all the property he had secured, whether provisions, metals, or precious stones, and distributed them among the troops, to carry them to the bottom of the mountain. When the infidels found that the Musulmans were retiring, they waited for them in the gorges of the mountain, and occupied the defiles before them. They cut down old trees, and cast them from the heights of the mountain, and these killed all with whom they came in contact. The greater part of the men perished, the rest were taken. The Hindus seized the treasures, merchandize, horses, and arms. Of all the Musulmans only three chiefs escaped—the commander Nakbia, Badru-d din Malik Daulat Shah, and a third whose name I have forgotten.

This disaster deeply affected the army of India, and weakened it in a marked manner. Soon afterwards the Sultan made peace with the inhabitants of the mountain, on condition of their paying him a certain tribute. They owned, in fact, the land at the foot of the mountain, and this they could not cultivate without the permission of the Sultan.

Rebellion of the Sharif Jalalu-d din in the Province of Ma'bar, etc.

The Sultan had appointed the *sharif*, Jalalu-d din Ahsan Shah, to be governor of the country of Ma'bar, which is at the distance of six months' journey from Dehli. This Jalalu-d din rebelled, usurped the ruling power, killed the lieutenants and agents of the Sovereign, and struck in his own name gold and silver money. On one side of the coins there was impressed the following (letters): *"toe* and *he, ye* and *sin,"* (these letters, which form the titles of the 20th and 26th chapters of the Kuran, are among the epithets bestowed upon Muhammad,) and (the words) "father of *fakirs* and of the indigent, the glory of the world and of religion." On the other face the following: "He who puts his trust in the help of the All-merciful, Ahsan Shah Sultan." The Sultan, when he was informed of this revolt, set forth to suppress it. * * *

Executions by means of Elephants

The elephants which execute men have their tusks covered with sharp irons, resembling the coulter of the plough which turns up the ground, and with edges like those of knives. The driver mounts the elephant, and, when a person is thrown in front, the animal winds his trunk round him, hurls him into the air, and, catching him on one of his tusks, dashes him to the ground, when he places one of his feet on the breast of the victim. After this he does as he is directed by his rider, under the orders of the Sultan. If the Sultan desires the culprit to be cut in pieces, the elephant executes the command by means of the irons above described; if the Sultan desires the victim to be left alone, the elephant leaves him on the ground, and (the body) is then stripped of its skin.

Campaign in Ma'bar

The Sultan arrived in the country of Tilang, and proceeded towards the province of Ma'bar, to repress the *sharif* of the country, who had rebelled. He halted at Badrakot, capital of Tilang, three months' march from Ma'bar. Pestilence then broke out in his army, and the greater part of it perished. * * * When the Sultan saw this calamity, he returned to Daulatabad. * * * On his journey he was taken ill, and the rumour spread that he was dead. * * * Amir Hushanj, when he heard this rumour, fled to an infidel prince named Burabrah, who dwelt in lofty mountains between Daulatabad and Kukan Tanah (Tana in the Konkan). * * *

Famine

Dearth made its appearance in various provinces, and the Sultan proceeded with his troops to encamp on the Ganges at ten days' journey from Dehli. [*Rebellion of 'Ainu-l Mulk.*] The *wazir* conducted (the prisoner) 'Ainu-l Mulk to the presence of the Sovereign. The rebel was mounted on a bull and was quite naked, saving only a scrap of stuff tied by a string round his waist. * * * The sons of the *amirs* surrounded the captive, insulted him, spat in his face, and buffeted his companions. * * * The Sultan directed that the prisoner should be dressed in clothes like those of conductors of pack-horses, that he should have four chains put upon his legs, that his hands should be fastened to his neck, and that he should be given into the custody of the *wazir*, Khwaja-i Jahan. * * * The Sultan returned to his capital after an absence of two years and a half. He pardoned 'Ainu-l Mulk.

During the time that the Sultan was absent from his capital in his expedition to Ma'bar, a famine arose and became serious. The *man* of wheat rose to sixty *dirhams* and more. Distress was general, and the position of affairs very grave. One day I went out of the city to meet the *wazir*, and I saw three women, who were cutting in pieces and eating the skin of a horse which had been dead some months. Skins were cooked and sold in the markets. When bullocks were slaughtered, crowds rushed forward to catch the blood, and consumed it for their sustenance. * * * The famine being unendurable, the Sultan ordered provisions for six months to be distributed to all the population of Dehli. The judges, secretaries, and officers inspected all the streets and markets, and supplied to every person provisions for half a year, at the rate of one pound and a half, Mughribi weight, each. * * *

Entry of the Sultan into Dehli

The Sovereign mounted his horse to enter his capital. * * * Over his head was carried a parasol, and before him was carried the *ghashiya*, or saddle-cloth, trimmed with gold and diamonds. Some small balistas were placed upon elephants, and as the Sultan approached the city, gold and silver pieces, mixed, were discharged from these machines among the people.

Appointment as Ambassador

After I had passed forty days in the hermitage, the Sultan sent me some saddled horses, slaves of both sexes, and clothes, and money for my expenses. I dressed myself, and went to wait upon the Sovereign. * * * When I arrived, he showed me greater honour than ever he had done before, and said, "I have sent for you to make you my ambassador to the King of China, for I know your love for voyages and travels." He furnished me with all that was necessary, and named the persons who were to go with me.

ON FIRE-WORSHIP IN UPPER INDIA

Nizamu-d din Ahmad mentions no other event of Ibrahim's reign but the following: "The Sultan turned his face towards Hindustan, and conquered many towns and forts, and amongst them was a city exceedingly populous, inhabited by a tribe of Khurasani descent, whom Afrasiyab had expelled from their native country. * * * It was so completely reduced by the power and perseverance of the Sultan, that he took away no less than 100,000 captives." Abu-l Fida and the *Tabakat-i Nasiri* are silent. The *Tarikh-i Alfi* says, "Ibrahim next marched against Derapur in Hindustan, a place which many great emperors found it impracticable to conquer. Several histories state that this place was inhabited by the descendants of the people of Khurasan, who for their disloyal and rebellious conduct had been long before banished from the country by Afrasiyab, Emperor of Turan." The *Muntakhabu-t Tawarikh* has nothing more on the subject than is contained in the *Tabakat-i Akbari*. The *Rauzatu-s Safa* is the same as the *Tarikh-i Alfi*, except that the former omits the name of the place. Firishta adds a few particulars not to be found in the others. He says:— "The King marched from thence to another town in the neighbourhood, called Dera, the inhabitants of which came originally from Khurasan, and were banished thither with their families by Afrasiyab, for frequent rebellions. Here they had formed themselves into a small independent state, and, being cut off from intercourse with their neighbours by a belt of mountains nearly impassable, had preserved their ancient customs and rites by not intermarrying with any other people. The King, having with infinite labour cleared a road for his army over the mountains, advanced towards Dera, which was well fortified. This place was remarkable for a fine lake of water about one *parasang* and a half in circumference, the waters of which did not apparently diminish, either from the heat of the weather or from being used by the army. At this place the King was overtaken by the rainy season; and his army, though greatly distressed, was compelled to remain before it for three months. But as soon as the rains abated, he summoned the town to surrender and acknowledge the faith. Sultan Ibrahim's proposal being rejected, he renewed the siege, which continued some weeks, with great slaughter on both sides. The town, at length, was taken by assault, and the Muhammadans found in it much wealth, and 100,000 persons, whom they carried in bonds to Ghazni. Some time after, the King accidentally saw one of those unhappy men carrying a heavy stone, with great difficulty and labour, to a palace which he was then building. This exciting his pity, he commanded the prisoner to throw it down and leave it there, at the same time giving him his liberty. This stone happened to be on the public road, and proved troublesome to passengers, but as the King's rigid enforcement of his commands was universally known, no one attempted to touch it. A courtier one day having stumbled with his horse over the stone, took occasion to mention it to the King, intimating that he thought it would be advisable to have it removed. To which the King replied, 'I commanded it to be thrown down and left there; and there it must remain as a monument of the calamities of war, and to commemorate my sense of its evils. It is better for a king to be pertinacious in the support even of an inadvertent command than that he should depart from his royal word.' The stone accordingly remained where it was; and was shown as a curiosity in the reign of Sultan Bairam several years afterwards."

The position of this place is very difficult to fix. Firishta says that in the year 472 H. Ibrahim marched in person to India, and conquered portions of it never before visited by the Musulmans. He extended his conquests to Ajodhan, now called Pattan Shaikh Farid Shakr Ganj. He then went to Rudpal, situated on the summit of a steep hill, which a river embraced on three sides, and which was protected by an impervious wood, infested by serpents. He then marched to Dera, which Briggs seems to place in the valley of the Indus, because he adds in a note, "Dera seems a common name in the vicinity of Multan for a town." The reading of the *Tarikh-i Alfi* with respect to the two first places is much the most probable,—namely, a fort in the country of Jud [1] and Damal.

The *Rauzatu-s Safa* does not mention the first place, and speaks of the second as if it were on the sea-shore. The third place he does not name. In Firishta it is Dera, and in the *Tarikh-i Alfi* Derapur. This would seem to be the place called Derabend, near Torbela, on the Upper Indus.[2] It is possible that the Dehra of Dehra Dun may be meant; but, though the belt of mountains, the inaccessible jungle, the seclusion of the inhabitants, and the identity of name, are in favour of this supposition, we are at a loss for the inexhaustible lake and the impregnability of the position.

All the authors, however, who mention the circumstance, whether they give the name or not, notice that the inhabitants were banished by Afrasiyab; and this concurrent tradition respecting their expulsion from Khurasan seems to indicate the existence of a colony of fire-worshippers in these hills, who preserved their peculiar rites and customs, notwithstanding the time which had elapsed since their departure from their native country.

Putting aside the probability, which has frequently been speculated upon, of an original connexion between

---

[1] This country is frequently mentioned by the early historians. It lies between the Indus and the Jallam, and is the Ayud of the old travellers. It is the old Sanskrit name, and occurs in the Puranic lists, and on the Allahabad pillar, under the name of *Yaudheya*. Wilford says it is the Hud of the Book of Esther. It occurs also in the marginal legend of the reverse of the Bactro-Pehlevi Coins. See *Journ. As. Soc. Bengal*, vol. vi. p. 973; *As. Researches*, vol. viii. p. 339; Lassen, *Zeitschrift f. d. K. d. Morgenlands*, vol. iii. p. 196.

[2] Vigne, *Kashmir*, vol. l. p. 122. See also Abbot's paper on Nikaia, *Journ. As. Soc. Bengal*, 1852.

the Hindu religion and the worship of fire,[2] and the derivation of the name of Magadha from the Magi, there is much in the practical worship of the Hindus, such as the *hom*, the *gayatri*, the address to the sun[3] at the time of ablution, the prohibition against insulting that luminary by indecent gestures,[4]—all which would lead an inattentive observer to conclude the two religions to bear a very close resemblance to one another. It is this consideration which should make us very careful in receiving the statements of the early Muhammadan writers on this subject; and the use of the word *Gabr*, to signify not only, especially, a fire-worshipper, but, generally, an infidel of any denomination, adds to the probability of confusion and inaccuracy.[5]

Khusru, in the *Khazainu-l Futuh* (p. 76), calls the sun the *kibla* of the Hindus, and it is quite evident that throughout his works *Gabr* is used as equivalent to Hindu. In one passage he speaks of the *Gabrs* as worshippers both of stones and fire.

European scholars have not been sufficiently attentive to this double use of the word, and all those who have relied upon M. Petis de la Croix's translation of Sharafu-d din, have considered that, at the period of

---

[2] *Calc. Rev.* vol. xxi. pp. 107, 128; *Mod. Trav., India*, vol. i. p. 120; Rampoldi, viii. p. 58; Mickle's *Camoens*, p. 356; Dr. Cox's *Sacred Hist. and Biog.*, p. 120; R. P. Knight's *Symbolic Language*, "Fire."

[3] See Wilson, *Rig-Veda*, Pref. pp. 28, 29, and *Index*, voce "Agni"; Elphinstone's *India*, vol. i. p. 78; also Lucian's description of the circular dance peculiar to Indian priests, in which they worship the sun, standing with their faces towards the east.—*De Saltationes*. See also Bohlen, *Das alte Indien*, vol. i. pp. 137, 146; Ersch and Gruber, *Encyclopädie der Wissenschaften und Kunste*, art. *Indien*, pp. 166, 172; Drummond's *Origines*, vol. III. p. 430.

[4] Hesiod enables us to disguise it in a learned language, *mēd ent esthioi tetrammenos orthos omikhelu.*
Op. et Di. v. 672.
See also Menu, iv. 52; Ramayana, ii. 59; Bohlen, *Das alte Ind.*, vol. i. p. 139; *Akhlak-i Jalali*, p. 293.

[5] "A Christian is called amongst them Gower, that is, unbeleever and uncleane, esteeming all to be infidels and pagans which do not believe as they do, in their false, filthie prophets, Mahomet and Murtezalli."—A. Jenkins. Hakluyt. vol. I. p. 391.

Timur's invasion, fire-worship prevailed most extensively in Upper India, because *Gabr* is used throughout by the historians of that invasion to represent the holders of a creed opposed to his own, and against which his rancour and cruelty were unsparingly directed. There is distinct mention in the *Matla'u-s Sa'dain* of fire-worshippers, as distinct from the Hindus; and the Kashmirians, according to Firishta, were fire-worshippers at the time of the Muhammadan invasion.¹ The men of Deogir are called fire-worshippers in the *Tarikh-i 'Alai*.

But though the word is used indiscriminately, there are certain passages in which it is impossible to consider that any other class but fire-worshippers is meant. Thus, it is distinctly stated in Timur's Memoirs, and by Sharafu-d din, that the people of Tughlikpur⁸ believed *in the two principles of good and evil in the universe, and acknowledged Ahriman and Yezdan (Ormuzd)*. The captives massacred at Loni⁹ are said to have been *Magians, as well as Hindus*, and Sharafu-d din states that the son of Safi the Gabr threw himself into the fire, *which he worshipped*.¹⁰

We cannot refuse our assent to this distinct evidence of the existence of fire-worshippers in Upper India as late as the invasion of Timur, A.D. 1398-9. There is, therefore, no improbability that the independent tribe which had been expelled by Afrasiyab, and practised their own peculiar rites, and whom Ibrahim the Ghaznivide attacked in A.D. 1079, were a colony of fire-worshippers from Iran, who, if the date assigned be true, must have left their native

---

¹ Briggs, vol. iv. p. 449.
⁸ [See Vol. III. pp. 431 and 494, and see the Editor's note upon this passage at page 506 of Vol. III. (Original Ed.). A further instance of the confusion of Brahmanical and Zoroastrian institutions may be found elsewhere, where Barauni, in treating upon Parsi fire-worship, declares the Hindu *hom* to be "a ceremony derived from fire-worship," evidently meaning Zoroastrianism.]
⁹ [See Vol. III. pp. 436 and 497.] (Original Ed.) Price's *Chronological Retrosp. of Mah. Hist.*, vol. iii, p. 254.
¹⁰ [See vol. III. p. 506.] (Original Ed.).

country before the reforms effected in the national creed by Zoroaster.

Indeed, when we consider the constant intercourse which had prevailed from the oldest time between Persia and India,[11] it is surprising that we do not find more unquestionable instances of the persecuted fire-worshippers seeking an asylum in Northern India as well as in Gujarat. The instances in which they are alluded to before this invasion of Timur are very rare, and almost always so obscurely mentioned as to leave some doubt in the mind whether foreign ignorance of native customs and religious rites may not have given a colour to the narrative.

The evidence of the Chinese traveller, Hiuen-thsang, to the existence of sun-worship at Multan in 640 A.D., is very decisive. He found there a "temple of the sun, and an idol erected to represent that grand luminary," with dwellings for the priests, and reservoirs for ablution;[12] yet he says the city was inhabited chiefly by men of the Brahmanical religion. A few centuries before, if Philostratus is to be believed, Apollonius, after crossing the Indus, visited the temple of the sun at Taxila, and Phraotes, the chief of the country, describes the Indians as in a moment of joy "snatching torches from the altar of the sun," and mentions that he himself never drank wine except "when sacrificing to the sun." After crossing the Hyphasis, Apollonius goes to a place, which would seem to represent Jwala Mukhi, where they "worship fire" and "sing hymns in honour of the sun."[13] When the Arabs arrived in the valley of the Indus, they found the same temple, the same idol, the same dwellings, the same reservoirs, as had struck the Chinese, but their description of the idol would lead us to suppose that it was a representation of Budh. Biruni, however, whose testimony is

---

[11] Troyer, *Raja Tarangini*, vol. ii. p. 441.
[12] *Journal Asiatique*, 4th series, tom. viii. p. 298, and *Foe Koue Ki*, p. 393.
[13] Philostrati *Vita Apollonii*, lib. ii. capp. 24. 32, lib. iii. cap. 14, ed. G. Olearius (Leip. 1709), pp. 77. 85, 103; *Hist. Sikhs* (Calc. 1846), p. 20.

more valuable than that of all other Muhammadans, as he was fully acquainted with the religious system of the Hindus, plainly tells us[14] that the idol of Multan was called *Aditya*,[15] because it was consecrated to the *sun*, and that Muhammad bin Kasim, the first invader, suspended a piece of cow's flesh from its neck, in order to show his contempt of the superstition of the Indians, and to disgust them with this double insult to the dearest objects of their veneration.[16]

Shortly before Biruni wrote, we have another instance of this tendency to combine the two worships. In the message which Jaipal sent to Nasiru-d din, in order to dissuade him from driving the Indians to desperation, he is represented to say, according to the *Tarikh-i Alfi*; "The Indians are accustomed to pile their property, wealth, and precious jewels in one heap, and to kindle it with the fire, *which they worship*. Then they kill their women and children, and with nothing left in the world they rush to their last onslaught, and die in the field of battle, so that for their victorious enemies the only spoil is dust and ashes." The declaration is a curious one in the mouth of a Hindu, but may perhaps be considered to indicate the existence of a modified form of pyrolatry in the beginning of the eleventh century. The practice alluded to is nothing more than the *Jauhar*, which is so frequently practised by Hindus in despair, and was not unknown to the nations of antiquity. Sardanapalus performed it, on the capture of Babylon. "He raised a large pyre in his palace, threw upon it all his wealth in

[14] M. Reinaud, *Fragments Arabes et Persans*, p. 143.
[15] See Lassen, *Indische Alterthumskunde*, vol. I. p. 781; *Anthologia Sanscritica*, p. 172; *As. Res.*, vol. I. p. 263; Vans Kennedy, *Ancient and Hindu Mythology*, p. 849.
[16] There is nothing in the various origins ascribed to the name of Multan which gives any colour to the supposition that the city was devoted to the worship of the sun; nor is there anything at present to indicate that worship. See Lassen, *Indische Alterthumskunde*, vol. i p. 99; *Zeitschrift f. d. K. d. Morg.*, vol. iii. p. 198; Mod, vol. i. pp. 69, 119; Reinaud's *Mem*, pp. 98, 100. The universality of Sun-worship is shown in Squier's *Serpent Symbol in America*, and Macrob, *Saturn*, i. c. 22.

gold, silver, and royal robes, and then placing his concubines and eunuchs on it, he, they, and the entire palace were consumed in the flames."[17] The Saguntines did the same, when their city was taken by Hannibal;[18] Juba also had prepared for a *Jauhar*,[19] and Arrian gives us an account of one performed by the Brahmans, without noticing it as a practice exclusively observed by that class.[20] The peculiarity of the relation consists in Jaipal's declaration that the Indians *worshipped the fire*, not in the fact of their throwing their property and valuables into it. The practice of self-cremation also appears to have been common at an earlier period; and there were conspicuous instances of it when foreign nations first became acquainted with India. One occurs in Vol. II. p. 27, where this very Jaipal, having no opportunity of dying in the field of battle, committed himself to the flames. Other histories tell us that it was then a custom amongst the Hindus that a king who had been twice defeated was disqualified to reign; and that Jaipal, in compliance with this custom, resigned his crown to his son, lighted his funeral pyre with his own hands, and perished in the flames. The Greeks and Romans were struck with the instances which they witnessed of the same practice. Calanus, who followed the Macedonian army from Taxila, solemnly burnt himself in their presence at Pasargadæ, being old and tired of his life.[21] Zarmanochegas, who accompanied the Indian ambassadors sent by

[17] Diodorus Siculus, II. 27. [18] Polybius, iii. 17; Livy, xxi. 14.
[19] Merivale vol. ii. p. 378; Cox's *Sacred Hist. and Biog.*, p. 242.
[20] *De Expedit. Alex.*, vi. 7. See also *Ency. Metr.*, "Rom Rep." and "Greece"; Herod. on the Syrians; Q. Curtius. ix. 14; Niebuhr's Lectures, vol. ii. pp. 82, 169, 247, 289; Michaud's *Crusades*, vol. i. p. 429; Layard's *Nineveh*, vol. ii. p. 218; Arnold, vol. iii. pp. 66, 429; *Mod. Univ. Hist.*, vol. iii. p. 195, xi. p. 68.

Quique suas struxera pyras, vivique calentes
Conscendere rogos. Proh! quanta est gloria genti
Injecisse manum fatis, vitaque repletos
Quod superest, donasse Diis.─────
Pharsalia, iii. 240.

[21] Diodorus Sic. xvii. 107; Valerius Max. I. viii. *Extern.* 10; Cicero, *Tusc.* ii. 22; Grier, 108, Index, v. "Calanus"; Elphinstone's *India*, vol. i. pp. 90, 461, 462, 471.

a chief, called Porus, to Augustus, burnt himself at Athens, and directed the following inscription to be engraved on his sepulchral monument:—"Here lies Zarmanochegas, the Indian of Bargosa, who deprived himself of life, according to a *custom prevailing among his countrymen.*"[21]

Strabo correctly observes, on the authority of Megasthenes, that suicide is not one of the dogmas of Indian philosophy; indeed, it is attended by many spiritual penalties:[22] and even penance which endangers life is prohibited.[24] There is a kind of exception, however, in favour of suicide by fire and water,[30] but then only when age, or infirmity, makes life grievous and burdensome. The former has of late years gone quite out of fashion, but it is evident that in ancient times there were many devotees ready to sacrifice themselves in that mode. It was, therefore, a habit sufficiently common amongst the Indians of that early period, to make Lucan remark upon it as a peculiar glory of that nation. All this, however, may have occurred without any reference to fire as an object of worship; but the speech of Jaipal, if not attributed to him merely through Muhammadan ignorance, shows an unquestionable devotion to that worship.

But to continue, Istakhri, writing a century earlier than this transaction, says, "Some parts of Hind and Sind belong to *Gabrs,* but a greater portion to Kafirs and idolaters; a minute description of these places would, therefore, be unnecessary and unprofitable."[26] Here, evidently, the fire-worshippers are alluded to as a distinct class; and these statements, written at different periods respecting the religious creeds of the Indians, seem calculated to impart a further degree of credibility to the

[21] Suetonius, *Augustus,* 21; Strabo, Geograph. xv. 1; Valentyn. vol. i. p. 60; Ritter, *Erdk.,* vol. iv. part I, p. 489.
[22] Rhode, *Religiose Bildung der Hindus,* vol. i. p. 451; Bohlen. *Das alte Indien,* vol. i. pp. 286-290; C. Muller, *Frag. Græc,* p. 139; his *Scrip. rerum Al. mag.* pp. 51, 57.
[24] See Wilson's note to Mill's *British India,* vol. ii. p. 417.
[25] Colebrooke, *Asiatic Researchs,* vol. vii. p. 256; where an instance is adduced from the *Raghuvansa* and *Ramayana.*
[26] Ouseley's *Oriental Geography,* p. 146.

specific assertions of Sharafu-d din, Khondamir, and the other historians of Timur's expedition to India. But the people alluded to by them need not have been colonies of refugees, fleeing from Muhammadan bigotry and persecution. There are other modes of accounting for their existence in these parts. They may have been Indian converts to the doctrine of Zoroaster, for we read that not only had he secret communication with the Brahmans of India,[37] but when his religion was fully established he endeavoured to gain proselytes in India, and succeeded in converting a learned Brahman, called Tchengrighatchah by Anquetil du Perron,[38] who returned to his native country with a great number of priests. Firdusi tells us that Isfendiyar[39] induced the monarch of India to renounce idolatry and adopt fire-worship, insomuch that not a Brahman remained in the idol-temples. A few centuries afterwards, we have indisputable testimony to the general spread of these doctrines in Kabul and the Panjab. The emblems of the Mithraic[40] worship so predominate on the coins of the Kanerkis, as to leave no

---

[37] Bactrianus Zoroastres, cum superioris Indiæ secreta fidentius penetraret, ad nemorosam quamdam venerat solitudinem, cujus tranquillis silentiis præcelsa Brachmanorum ingenia potiuntur: eorumque monitu rationes mundani motus et siderum, purosque sacrorum ritus, quantum colligere potuit, eruditus, ex his, quæ didicit, aliqua sensibus Magorum infudit.—Ammian. Marcell. *Juliana*, xxiii. 6, 33. See *Anc. Univ. Hist.*, vol. iv. p. 301; Guigniaut's *Notes to Creuzer's Religions*, tom. i. pp. 689, 690.

[38] *Zendavesta*, vol. i. ch. 2, p. 70.

[39] He is said, according to the *Zinatu-l Tawarikh*, to have been the first convert made by Zoroaster, and Gushtasp, his father, was persuaded by the eloquence of the prince to follow his example. The king ordered twelve thousand cow-hides to be tanned fine, in order that the precepts of his new faith might be engrossed upon them. In this respect what a contrast is there to Hindu exclusiveness! The Pandits withheld their sacred books from Col. Polier, for fear that he should bind them in calf-skin. Polier, *Mythologie des Indous*, tom. II. p. 224; Ovid, *Fasti*, i. 629; Riley,*p. 40.

[40] Using this word in its usual, though not proper, acceptation. The real Mithraic worship was a fusion of Zoroastrianism and Chaldaism, or the Syrian worship of the sun. See the authorities quoted in Guizot's and Milman's notes to Gibbon's *Decline and Fall*, vol. I. p. 340; *Anc. Univ. Hist.*, vol. iv. pp. 150, 157.

doubt upon the mind that it was the state-religion of that dynasty.[11]

Ritter entertains the supposition, that as the Khilji family came from the highlands which afforded a shelter to this persecuted race, they may have had a leaning to these doctrines, and he offers a suggestion, that the new religion which 'Alau-d din wished to promulgate may have been that of Zoroaster,[12] and that this will account for the Panjab and the Doab being full of his votaries at the time of Timur's invasion. But this is a very improbable supposition, and he has laid too much stress upon the use of the word *Gabr*, which, if taken in the exclusive sense adopted by him, would show not only that these tracts were entirely occupied by fire-worshippers, but that Hindus were to be found in very few places in either of them.

After this time, we find little notice of the prevalence of fire-worship in Northern India ; and its observers must then have been exterminated, or they must have shortly after been absorbed into some of the lower Hindu communities. Badauni, however, mentions the destruction of fire-altars one hundred years later by Sultan Sikandar in A.H. 910. It may not be foreign to this part of the inquiry to remark, that Abu-l Fazl speaks of the *Gubree* language as being one of the thirteen used in the *suba* of Kabul (*Ain-i Akbari*, vol. ii. p. 1265). The *Gubree* language is also mentioned in Babar. There is a "Gubber" hill and pass not far from Bunnoo, inhabited by the Battani tribe ; and on the remotest borders of Rohilkhand, just under the hills, there is a tribe called *Gobri*, who retain some peculiar customs, which seem to have no connexion with Hindu superstition. They are said to have preceded the present occupants of the more cultivated lands to the south of the Tarai, and may possibly be the descendants of some of the *Gabrs* who found a refuge in Upper India.

[11] Lassen, Journ. As. Soc. Bengal, vol. ix. p. 456, and H. T. Prinsep. *Note on the Histor. Results from Bactrian Coins*, p. 108.
[12] See Ritter, *Erdkunde von Asien*, vol. iv. part 1. pp. 577-79.

The name of *Gobri* would certainly seem to encourage the notion of identity, for the difference of the first vowel, and the addition of a final one, offer no obstacle, any more than they do in the name of *Gobryas*,[a] who gave information to Socrates on the subject of the Persian religion, and is expressly declared by Plato to be an *aner magos*. According to J. Cunningham, there is a wild tribe called *Magyas* between Malwa and Gujarat, who are used as *shikaris*. They are supposed to have been fire-worshippers, but they have no pyrolatrous observances at present.

There is another inferior Hindu tribe, to the west of the upper Jumna, and in the neighbourhood of the Tughlikpur mentioned above, who, having the name of *Mugh*,[b] and proclaiming themselves of foreign extraction (inasmuch as they are descendants of Raja Mukhtesar, a Sarsuti Brahman, King of Mecca, and maternal grand-father of Muhammad!!),[c] would seem to invite

---

[a] Plato, *Axiochus*, Tauchnitz, vol. viii. p. 204. The same name is common in Herodotus, Xenophon, Justin, and other authors, who deal in Persian History. The warmth of an Irish imagination ascribes to the Greeks a still greater perversion of the original word.

"Hyde," says the enthusiastic O'Brien, "was the only one who had any idea of the composition of Cabiri, when he declared it was a Persian word somewhat altered from Gabri or Guebri, and signifying fire-worshippers. It is true that Gabri now stands for fire worshippers, but that is only because they assumed to themselves this title, which belonged to another order of their ancestors. The word is derived from *gabh*, a smith, and *ir*, sacred, meaning the sacred smiths, and Cabiri being only a perversion of it, is of course in substance of the very same import. * * * Gobhan Saer means the sacred poet, or the Freemason Sage, one of the Guebhres, or Cabiri."—*Round Towers of Ireland*, pp. 354, 355. See *Journ. Roy. As. Soc.*, vol. xi. pp. 134-5.

[b] *Journ. As. Soc. Bengal*, vol. vii. p. 764.

[c] See Quatremere's observations in the *Journal des Savants*, January, 1851. This is not at all an uncommon paternity for the lower tribes to assume. There is nothing in which Hindu ignorance is more betrayed, than in these silly attempts to enrol the false prophet amongst their native heroes. See especially Wilford's absurd and dirty story, showing how Muhammad was of Brahmanical descent. (*As. Res.* vol. ix. p. 160). Wilson considers that the story was manufactured especially for Wilford, but it is traditionally current among the ignorant in some parts of Upper India. (*Note to Mill's India*, vol. ii. p. 176.) The reputed Brahmanical origin of Akbar is more reasonable, inasmuch as it can be attributed to

the attention of any inquirer after the remnant of the stock of Magians; but all their customs, both religious and social, are of the Hindu stamp, and their only peculiarity consists in being the sole caste employed in the cultivation of *mendhi* (Lawsonia inermis).[34]

gratitude, and is not opposed to the doctrine of transmigration; but why Muhammud should also be chosen, whose votaries have proved the most unrelenting persecutors of Hindus, can only be ascribed to the marvellous assimilating powers of their mental digestion, fostered by the grossest credulity and ignorance of past events, which can, as Milton says, "corporeal to incorporeal turn," and to that indiscriminate craving after adaptation, which induce them even now to present their offerings at the shrines of Muhammadans, whose only title to saint is derived from the fact of their having despatched hundreds of infidel and accursed Hindus to the nethermost pit of Hell.

[34] See also Shea and Troyer, *Dabistan*, vol. i. pp. c. cxxv.; *Asiatic Researches*, vol. ix. pp. 74, 81, 212, vol. xi. p. 76, vol. xvi. p. 15; Dr. Bird *Journ. As. Soc. Bombay*, no. ix. p. 186; Rammohun Roy, *Translation of the Veds*, pp. 29, 73, 109-118; Malcolm, *History of Persia*, vol. i. pp. 488-094; Wilson, *Vishnu Purana*, pp. xl. 84, 397; *North British Review*, no. ll. p. 376; Klaproth, *Memoires Relatifs a l'Asie*, tom. ii. p. 81; Ouseley, *Travels in Persia*, vol. i. pp. 102-146; Ritter, *Erdkunde von Asien*, vol. iv. pt. i. pp. 489, 574, 614-619; Rhode, *Religiose Bildung der Hindus*, vol. i. p. 42, vol. ii. p. 290; Moor's *Hindu Pantheon*, pp. 295-302; Colebrooke, *Miscellaneous Essays*, vol. i. pp. 30, 149, 155, 188, 217; F. Creuzer, *Symbolik und Mythologie*, vol. i. pp. 518-524; Reinaud's *Memoire's sur l'Inde*, *passim*; Reinaud's *Fragments Arabes et Persans*, p. 46; Elphinstone's *History of India*, vol. i. pp. 78, 90, 461-2, 471, 489; *Journal of the Asiatic Society of Bengal*, 1840, pp. 105-7, 1852, p. 447; *Journ. Roy. Asiatic Society*, vol. xii. pp. 26, 27; *Calcutta Review*, vol. xxi. p. 150, vol. xxv. p. 45; Grote's *Greece*, vol. iv. p. 299, vol. v. p. 397; J. H. Hottingeri *Thesaurus Philologicus seu Clavis Scripturæ*, 1649, p. 56; Buxtorf, *Lex.*, p. 704; *Mod. Trav. in India*, vol. i. p. 145, vol. iv. pp. 201 to 205; Tod. vol. i. pp. 102, 112, 217, 282; Fergusson's *Anc. Arch. Hind.*, p. 6; R. S. Poole's *Horæ Egyptiacæ*, p. 205; Cory's *Ancient Fragments*, p. 272; Maisey's *Report on Sanchi Topes*, Note B; Cunningham's *Bhilsa Topes*.

ON THE KNOWLEDGE OF SANSKRIT BY MUHAMMADANS

It is a common error to suppose that Faizi (v. p. 479) was the first[1] Muhammadan who mastered the difficulties of the Sanskrit,—that language, "of wonderful structure, more perfect than Greek, more copious than Latin, and more exquisitely refined than either."

Akbar's freedom from religious bigotry, his ardent desire for the cultivation of knowledge, and his encouragement of every kind of learning, and especially his regard for his Hindu subjects, imparted a stimulus to the cultivation of Indian literature, such as had never prevailed under any of his predecessors. Hence, besides Faizi, we have amongst the Sanskrit translators of his reign 'Abdu-l Kadir, Nakib Khan, Mulla Shah Muhammad, Mulla Shahri, Sultan Haji, Haji Ibrahim, and others. In some instances it may admit of doubt, whether the translations may not have been made from versions previously done into Hindi, oral or written. The word Hindi is ambiguous when used by a Muhammadan of that period. Nizamu-d din Ahmad, for instance, says that 'Abdu-l Kadir translated several works from the *Hindi*. Now, we know that he translated, amongst other works, the *Ramayana* and the *Singhasan Battisi*.[2] It is much more probable that these were in the original Sanskrit, than in Hindi. 'Abdu-l Kadir and Firishta tell us that the *Mahabharata* was translated into Persian from the *Hindi*, the former[3] ascribing the work chiefly to Nakib Khan, the

---

[1] Elphinstone's *History of India*, vol. ii. p. 317; *Biographical Dictionary*, L.U.K., vol. i. p. 585; Dow's *Hindoostan*, vol. i. p. 6; Briggs, vol. iv. p. 451. Gladwin mentions translations made before the time of Akbar in the *Ain-i Akbari*, vol. i. p. 103, vol. ii. p. 158.

[2] [See *supra*.]

[3] His account, which will be seen elsewhere, is very confused, and it is not easy to gather from it what share each of the coadjutors had in the translation. The same names are given in the *Ain-i Akbari*; Sprenger's *Bibl.*, pp. 59, 68.

latter to Faizi.⁴ Here again there is every probability of the Sanskrit being meant. In another instance, 'Abdu-l Kadir tells us that he was called upon to translate the *Atharva Veda* from the *Hindi*, which he excused himself from doing on account of the exceeding difficulty of the style and abstruseness of meaning, upon which the task devolved upon Haji Ibrahim Sirhindi, who accomplished it satisfactorily. Here it is evident that nothing but Sanskrit could have been meant.⁵ But though the knowledge of Sanskrit appears to have been more generally diffused at this time, it was by no means the first occasion that Muhammadans had become acquainted with that language. Even if we allowed that they obtained the abridgment of the *Pancha Tantra*, under the name of Fables of Bidpai, or *Hitopadesa,* through the medium of the Pehlevi,⁶ there are other facts which make it equally certain that the Muhammadans had attained a correct knowledge of the Sanskrit not long after the establishment of their religion ; even admitting, as was probably the case, that most of the Arabic translations were made by Indian foreigners resident at Baghdad.

In the *Khalifate* of Al-Mamun, the Augustan age of Arabian literature, the treatise⁷ of Muhammad bin Musa on Algebra, which was translated by Dr. Rosen in 1831; and the medical treatises of Mikah and Ibn Dahan, who are represented to be Indians,⁸ show that Sanskrit must have been well known at that time ; and even before that,

---

⁴ The author of the *Siyaru-l Muta-akhkhirin* (vol. I.) ascribes it to 'Abdul-l Kadir and Shaikh Muhammad Sultan Thanesari. The name of the translator is not mentioned in Abu-l Fazl's preface, but the work is said to have been done by several men of both religions.

⁵ In the *Ashika* and *Nuh-sipahr* of Amir Khusru there are two important passages, showing that in the former Hindi means Sanskrit ; and Amir Khusru in the same work says that he himself had a knowledge of the language.

⁶ See Memoire prefixed to S. de Sacy's edition of *Calilah wa Dimnah*, Paris, 1816. See also *Biographie Universelle,* tom. xxi. p. 471

⁷ Colebrooke, *Miscellaneous Essays*, vol. II. pp. 444-500.

⁸ *Biographical Dictionary*, L. U. K., vol. ii. p. 242.

the compilations of *Charaka* and *Susruta*[9] had been translated, and had diffused a general knowledge of Indian medicine amongst the Arabs. From the very first, we find them paying particular attention to this branch of science, and encouraging the profession of it so much, that two Indians, Manka and Salih, by name,—the former of whom translated a treatise on poison into Persian,—held appointmens as body-physicians at the Court of Harunu-r Rashid.[10] The Arabians possessed during the early periods of the *Khalifate* several other Indian works which had been translated into Arabic, some on astronomy,[11] some on music,[12] some on judicial astrology,[13] some on interpretation of dreams,[14] some on the religion and theogony of the Hindus,[15] some on their sacred scriptures,[16] on the calculation of nativities,[17] some on agriculture,[18] some on poisons,[19] some on physiognomy,[20] and some on

---

[9] Dietz, *Analecta Medica*, pp. 128-140.

[10] *Journal of Education*, vol. viii. p. 176; Royle, *Antiquity of Hindu Medicine*, p. 64; *Oriental Mag.*, March, 1823; D'Herbelot, arts. *Ketab al Samoum* and *Mangheh*; Abu'l Faragii, *Hist. Dynast.*, p. 238; Dietz, p. 124; Price, vol. ii. p. 88; *Biog. Dic.*, L. U. K., vol ii. p. 500; *Journ. Roy. As. Soc.*, vol. vi. p. 107; Reinaud's *Aboulfeda*, vol. i. p. 42; Rampoldi, vol. iv. pp. 451, 478; *Mod. Univ. Hist.*, vol. ii. p. 155; Cosmos (Sabine), vol. ii. notes 328, 340-1, 350-5-6; Wustenfeld, *Arab Aertza*, p. 19; Ritter, *Erdkunde*, vol. iv. part 1, pp. 529, 626.

[11] Casiri, *Bibliotheca Escurialensis*, vol. i. p. 240.

[12] Casiri, ibid., p. 427.

[13] Hottinger, *Promptuarium*, p. 254; Reinaud's *Aboulfeda*, vol. I. pp. 42, 46, 49.

[14] Casiri, *Bibliotheca Escurialensis*, vol. I. p. 401.

[15] Gieldemeister, *de rebus Indicis Scriptt. Arabb.*, pp. 104-119; De Guignes, *Mem. de l' Academ. des Inscript.*, tom. xxvi. p. 791 et seq.

[16] D' Herbelot, Arts. *Anbertkend*, *Ambahoumatah*, *Bahargiv*. See also *Ketab alkhafi*, *Ketab Roi al Hendi*, and several other articles under *Ketab*. Rampoldi, vol. iv. p. 328.

[17] Haji Khalfa, vol. I. p. 282; Dietz, *Analecta Medica*, p. 118; D'Herbelot, art. *Cancah*.

[18] Gildemeister, ix.

[19] Dietz, p. 118; D'Herbelot, *Ketab Roi al Hendi*.

[20] D'Herbelot, *Biblioth. Or.*, tom. iv. p. 725; Diez, *Analecta Medica*, p. 117.

palmistry,[21] besides others, which need not be here enumerated.

If we turn our eyes towards India, we find that scarcely had these ruthless conquerors gained a footing in the land, than Biruni exerted himself with the utmost diligence to study the language, literature, and science of India, and attained, as we have already seen, such proficiency in it, as to be able to translate into, as well as from, the Sanskrit. Muhammad bin Israil-al Tanukhi also travelled early into India, to learn the system of astronomy which was taught by the sages of that country.[22] There seems, however, no good authority for Abu-l Fazl's statement in the *Ain-i Akbari*,[23] that Abu Ma'shar (Albumazar) visited Benares at an earlier period :—and the visit of Ibn-al Baithar to India, four centuries afterwards, rests solely on the authority of Leo Africanus.[24]

Again, when Firoz Shah, after the capture of Nagarkot, in the middle of the fourteenth century, obtained possession of a valuable Sanskrit Library, he ordered a work on philosophy, divination, and omens to be translated, under the name of *Dalail-i Firoz-shahi*, by Maulana 'Izzu-d din Khalid Khani,—and to have enabled the translator to do this, he must have acquired no slight knowledge of the original, before his selection for the duty.

In the Nawwab Jalalu-d daula's Library at Lucknow, there is a work on astrology, also translated from the Sanskrit into Persian in Firoz Shah's reign. A knowledge of Sanskrit must have prevailed pretty generally about this time, for there is in the Royal Library at Lucknow a work on the veterinary art, which was translated from the Sanskrit by order of Ghiyasu-d din Muhammad Shah Khilji. This rare book, called *Kurrutu-l Mulk*, was translated as early as A.H. 783 (A.D. 1381), from an original, styled *Sala-*

---

[21] Haji Khalfa, vol. I. p. 263.
[22] Casiri, *Bibl. Escurial.*, vol. I. p. 439.
[23] *Ain-i Akbari*, vol. ii. p. 288 ; Gildemeister, 79.
[24] Hottingeri, *Bibl. quadrup.* ap. Gildemeister. *Scriptt. Arabb.*, pp. 6, 289, 316, 336.

tar, which is the name of an Indian, who is said to have been a Brahman, and the tutor of Susruta. The Preface says that the translation was made "from the barbarous Hindi into the refined Persian, in order that there may be no more need of a reference to infidels." It is a small work, comprising only 41 pages 8vo. of 13 lines, and the style is very concise. It is divided into eleven chapters and thirty sections. The precise age of this work is doubtful, because, although it is plainly stated to have been translated in A.H. 783, yet the reigning prince is called Sultan Ghiyasu-d din Muhammad Shah, son of Mahmud Shah, and there is no king so named whose reign exactly corresponds with that date. The nearest is Ghiyasu-d din 'Azim Shah bin Sikandar Shah, who reigned in Bengal from A.H. 769 to 775.[55] If Sultan Ghiyasu-d din Tughlik be meant, it should date sixty years earlier, and if the King of Malwa who bore that name be meant, it should be dated 100 years later; any way, it very much precedes the reign of Akbar.[56] The translator makes no mention in it of the work on the same subject, which had been previously translated from the Sanskrit into Arabic at Baghdad, under the name of *Kitabu-l Baitarat*.

From all these instances it is evident that Faizi did not occupy the entirely new field of literature for which he usually obtains credit.[57] The same error seems to

---

[55] There is something respecting this reign in the History of Mecca which relates to India, and shows great communication between Bengal and Arabia.

[56] It is curious, that without any allusion to this work, another on the veterinary art, styled *Salotari*, and said to comprise in the Sanskrit original 16,000 *slokas*, was translated in the reign of Shah Jahan, "when there were many learned men who knew Sanskrit," by Saiyid 'Abdu-lla Khan Bahadur Firoz Jang, who had found it amongst some other Sanskrit books, which during his expedition against Mewar, in the reign of Jahangir, had been plundered from Amar Singh, Rana of Chitor, and "one of the chief *zamindars* of the hill-country." It is divided into twelve chapters, and is more than double the size of the other.

[57] Faizi's *Lilavati* has many omissions, and the translation in some passage departs so far from the original "as induces the suspicion that Faizi contented himself with writing down the verbal explanation afforded by his assistants."—Dr. Taylor's *Lilavati*, p. 2.

have prevaded the history of European scholarship in Sanskrit. We read as early as A.D. 1677, of Marshall's being a proficient in the language, and without mentioning the dubious names of Anquetil du Perron[28] and Father Paolino,[29] others could be named, who preceded in this arduous path the celebrated scholars of the present period. Thus, Holwell says that he read and understood Sanskrit, and P. Pons, the Jesuit (1740), knew the language. In such an inquiry as this also must not be omitted the still more important evidence afforded by the *Mujmalu-t Tawarikh*, from which Extracts have been given in Vol. I. p. 100. (Original edition).

[28] See *Geschichte der Philosophie*, vol. I. p. 412; *Edinb. Rev.*, vol. I. p. 75; Heeren's *Historical Researches*, vol. ii. p. 129, and *Calcutta Review*, vol. xxiv. p. 471.

[29] Bohlen speaks of his *Grammatica Samscredamica*, Rom. 1790, as "full of the greatest blunders;" Sir William Jones designates him as "homo trium litterarum," and Leyden is even less complimentary in his strictures : "The publication of his *Vyacarana*, Rom. 1804, has given a death-blow to his vaunted pretensions to profound Oriental learning, and shown, as was previously suspected, that he was incapable of accurately distinguishing Sanskrit from the vernacular languages of India. Equally superficial, inaccurate, and virulent in his invective, a critic of his own stamp would be tempted to retort on him his own quotation from Ennius :—

Simia quam similis turpissima bestia vobis."

See *Das alte Indien*, vol. ii. p. 471 ; *As. Res.*, vol. x. p. 278 ; *Journ. Asiatique*, tom. ii. p. 218 ; Heeren, *Histor. Res.*, vol. ii. p. 108 ; M. Abel-Remusat, *Nouv. Mel. Asiat.*, tom. ii. pp. 305-315 ; *Quart. Or. Mag.*, vol. iv. p. 158.

[Addition to the note on the Autobiography of Timur in Vol. IV. p. 559. (Or. Ed.)

Since the publication of Vol. IV., (Or. Ed.) I have had access to a copy of the first volume of the *Matla'u-s Sa'dain* belonging to Professor Cowell; but I have not discovered in it any reference to the works from which the author drew his life of Timur.

Timur's "Testament" is given in the *Zafar-nama*, so the statement in p. 562 of Vol. IV. (Or. Ed.) requires correction.—J. D.]

www.ingramcontent.com/pod-product-compliance
Lightning Source LLC
Chambersburg PA
CBHW030354170426
43202CB00010B/1366